A growing number of people enter polygamy each year.

To understand contemporary polygamy, one needs to see into the minds of these women. To understand the men in polygamy, one needs to study their need of power, dominance, and the male sex drive. To understand the polygamous sects, one must study their leadership, a theocracy more political than religious. Each sect is a monarchy ruled by a despot who is a juggler of love and fear, molding and manipulating the true believer to his advantage.

Travel that world through a fictitious modern day family that leaves traditional Mormonism and enters polygamy, the father excited, the mother and teenagers deeply troubled. Meet the adult and teenage cliques of the governing "elite" families, the "second-class" families, the "obedient" women who believe they must be subservient in every way, and finally the strong-willed women who use their intrinsic powers to develop a life of freedom and choice within the group. Meet the men and their different uses of religious power over the women whose lives they control—*and those they only think they control.* In the end will these teenagers and their mother give up the "good life" they have created— and their very freedom?

With a law enforcement investigator's objective eye, Llewellyn explores the positives and negatives of this lifestyle. A Mormon, he came to believe the 1800s doctrine of plural marriage, entered polygamy, lived the life for many years, and then chose to leave. As additional research, he interviewed many people: men and women still in polygamy, women who have left, and teenagers who had the option to leave, and did.

Other Agreka™ Books About Polygamy

Murder of a Prophet: The Dark Side of Utah Polygamy
   by John Llewellyn – Fact-based Fiction

One Wife Too Many: Whispers of Margaret McConnell 1841-1898
   by Guenavere A. Sandberg – Non Fiction

A Teenager's Tears

When Parents Convert To Polygamy

Inspired by Actual Events

John R. Llewellyn

A Teenager's Tears: When Parents Convert To Polygamy
By John R. Llewellyn

© 2001 by John R. Llewellyn

First Edition

Library of Congress Catalog Card Number: 00-108807
ISBN: 188810659X

Cover design Lea Taylor
Cover Illustration Arianna Alexis

800 360-5284
www.agreka.com

John Llewellyn

Mr. Llewellyn's first fact-based novel *Murder of a Prophet: Dark Side of Utah Polygamy* has infuriated priesthood leaders of several polygamy groups and has been banned. *Salt Lake Tribune* writer Greg Burton stated in a front page review of the book, "Llewellyn is everything he purports to be and more. . ."

In the same article Rowena Erickson, a former polygamous wife who fled Utah's Kingston clan and later helped form a support group called Tapestry Against Polygamy is quoted, "I kept looking at the women and the girls he writes about and how real they are. He knows the life."

Investigator John R. Llewellyn was a deputy sheriff for twenty-three years in the Salt Lake County Sheriff's Office. Considered an expert, he spent a number of years in prolonged investigation of polygamy cults. He was often placed on loan to do special investigations for the County Attorney, District Attorney, and Attorney General.

Conducting the preliminary investigation of mass murderer Ervil LeBaron, who was convicted of ordering the murder of Dr. Rulon C. Allred in 1977, Deputy Llewellyn complied an extensive intelligence profile of the infamous polygamist. He also assisted French, British, and local television companies—all wanting to film documentaries—in making contact with appropriate members of polygamous groups. Mr. Llewellyn writes feature articles on the subject for newspapers and magazines.

The author pioneered the Morals Squad of the Sheriff Department, which handled the investigation of polygamous complaints. He also wrote a sex crimes manual for the Utah State Police Academy, where he taught Sex Crime Investigation, Interview, and Interrogation.

Preface

The publication of *Murder of a Prophet, The Dark Side of Utah Polygamy* outraged the Mormon fundamentalist subculture, who feared the book portrayed all polygamous men as exploiters, potential murderers, and female abusers. In Colorado City and Hildale the book was banned. In opposition to this book, three matriarchs in the polygamy subculture decided to publish a book of their own that showed the positive side of polygamy. They circulated a proposal to several hundred polygamous women explaining their objective and asked them to contribute anecdotes showing the positive side of polygamy to counter what had been written about the "occasional" bad side. Contributors were told their names would be kept confidential.

I personally know two of the women; both are intelligent and outstanding writers. As women and mothers, I rank them among the best, and as representatives of plural marriage, they are more virtuous, knowledgeable and spirited than most polygamous men. I wished them the best, and told them it is the women and not the men who ought to hold the priesthood keys because women in general are more gutsy, intellectually superior, and morally better equipped. I believe women are more capable of managing the polygamous groups. If they were in charge, there would be less larceny, less spouse abuse, fewer child molests, deception would decline and subterfuge held to a minimum.

As a former polygamist for a number of years during my adult life, I make no apologies or excuses for my past involvement. I received many personal blessings as an active polygamist, and I learned a great deal more about myself and how various people handle religion. I don't recommend the lifestyle to others, and I discourage my children from following in my footsteps. The lifestyle is severe, demanding, exhausting, cruel at times, and contains some unsavory leadership predators who take advantage of good and well meaning people.

Introduction

In the Allred Group, known as Apostolic United Brethren, of the children born in the "principle" of plural marriage, many more leave than stay. For example, of 48 children sired by the late Rulon C. Allred, only about 17 stayed in the principle. This figure is consistent with the other large polygamous groups. In talking with leading members of the Allred Group, they estimated that between 65 and 80 percent of their children apostatize.

A few of these dissident children contacted me after reading my novel, *Murder of a Prophet*. Their stories, together with my own observation and experiences, inspired me to contact other dissident children and write a second fact-based novel explaining why so many of these children leave. Their stories deserve to be told.

Apostolic United Brethren, the least oppressive sect of them all, is the basic model for my new novel, but I have also incorporated events and incidents from the other major groups, and from independent polygamists who belong to no group. I have created fictitious characters to represent the various types of teens and adults found in polygamy.

Visualize, if you will, what it would be like for an attractive, seventeen-year-old girl to have her parents suddenly join a polygamous sect. It happened to Emma. One day her life was normal, the next day she was thrust into a polygamous subculture. Emma's experiences, and the experiences of her friends, are typical of hundreds of young people living in cult-like Mormon polygamist sects.

The story is told from Emma's point of view, and from her perspective she sees little of the polygamous lifestyle to be desired. But as she moves about in the culture, she meets girls and women who find plural marriage desirable, secure, spiritual, and compatible in ways that satisfy their present needs and desires. If it were not so, there wouldn't be so many of them.

Women are the backbone and adhesive element that is indispensable to the success of polygamy. Many find plural marriage enriching, adventurous, more free and rewarding than monogamy. However, in some groups women are brainwashed and herded around until cut out like cattle. Others are skillfully programmed with inferiority complexes, making them dependent upon unscrupulous, lecherous leaders. Still others are raised in isolation making them ill-equipped to compete and survive in a modern cosmopolitan society. Some are by nature content to allow what they perceive as powerful, righteous men to take control of their lives.

To understand contemporary polygamy, one needs to see into the minds of these women. To understand the men in polygamy, one needs to study their need of power, dominance, and the male sex drive. To understand the polygamous sects, one must study their leadership, a theocracy more political than religious. Each sect is a monarchy ruled by a despot who is a juggler of love and fear, molding and manipulating the true believer to his advantage.

As of this writing, the media reports that the priesthood leader of one of the most oppressive polygamous groups has commanded that all of its children presently in the public school system must drop out and attend the group's private school or be home schooled. Additionally, he has commanded that any of their members who are teachers in the public school system must resign their jobs.

Members are commanded they must sever all ties with family or friends not in the group. It is reported that leaders recently chastised girls for ignoring the dress code of high collars, long skirts, and no pierced ears or makeup. Over the last twelve months, a half-dozen teenagers have been arrested for alcohol or tobacco violations, and reports about runaways continue. Some experts believe the leaders are fearful the next generation will be lost to the modern world or to the mainstream Church of Jesus Christ of Latter-day Saints, which disavowed polygamy 110 years ago.

Mike King, special investigator for the Utah attorney general and whose work a decade ago led to the arrest and conviction of polygamous child abuser Arvin Shreeve, stated that the tactics of this group come down to dominion, control and power.

Chapter One

The houses, trees, alfalfa fields, and telephone posts slipped past in a blur as the maroon Ford Explorer cruised southward on the rural Utah road. Gene spoke reassuringly as he drove, hoping to put Emma at ease. She slouched in the passenger seat next to her father and stared out the window, dreading the meeting she was about to attend, fighting an overwhelming depression.

Emma was in a state of shock. One day she was making plans with her friends, looking forward to the local church dance, and the next day she was told she was now a polygamist.

She fought her defiance and disbelief, wanting to shout at her dad, "I DON'T WANT TO BE A POLYGAMIST!"

But she didn't cry out. As a well brought up Mormon child, taught that obedience is an indispensable law of heaven, she sat next to her father, listening as he explained one more time how wonderful and special it was to be a polygamist child. "You'll meet lots of new friends," he said. "The girls your age are very friendly, modest, and chaste. They're the most virtuous girls in the world."

Emma, a vivacious seventeen-year-old, had no idea her parents had been studying plural marriage until a week ago one Sunday morning when they summoned their children to the family room for a meeting. Emma was dressed for Sunday School, eager to see her friends at church. Keith, twelve, plopped down in the rocker, tossing his basketball in the air, his red tie hanging crooked, his hair wet and plastered flat on his head. Emma's mother sat on the sofa next to her husband.

Emma immediately felt the tension. *Someone must have died.* Respectfully sobering to the occasion, Emma quietly sat nearby, spread her dress appropriately over her knees, and waited for the news. She had spent the last hour in the bathroom applying just the right amount of eye shadow and mascara to enrich her naturally dark eyes. A beautiful girl, she had inherited her mother's dimples and auburn hair.

Gene, dressed in his gray suit, white shirt and dark tie, took a deep breath and glanced at Connie, his wife. Her blank gaze gave him no encouragement. He turned to the children, "This is the last Sunday we'll be going to church in this ward."

"What!" Emma stammered.

"But, Dad, all my friends are here!" Keith exploded.

"We'll be moving soon and going to a new church," their father explained.

Emma looked at her mother's pale face. She knew there was more.

"You'll make new friends, Keith," Gene said, "lots of new friends who think and live like we do."

"My friends already think like I do," Keith retaliated.

Emma interrupted. "Dad, I don't understand. Why are we moving?"

He glanced at his wife.

Taking a deep breath he said, "You're going to have to trust me on this, kids. For the last five months your mother and I have been studying the original doctrine of our Church, before the government stepped in, and we've decided to make a major change in our lives." The children stared.

"Emma, listen to me," her father said in a tone of loving, but insistent, authority. "Do you believe that Joseph Smith was a prophet?"

"Yes," she answered hesitantly. For as long as Emma could remember, in church and at home, she had been told Joseph Smith was a prophet.

"Did you know that Joseph Smith had more than one wife?" he asked.

She looked at him, bewilderment in her brown eyes. "No!" Of course she had heard, but it was like a joke, something that had occurred in another time period.

Emma looked at her mother's ashen face.

The blood drained out of Emma. *Oh God*. Dizziness swept over her.

"Daddy," she whispered, "what are you trying to say?" But

deep inside Emma already knew. She could see it written all over her mother's face, eyes sunk deep, colorless tight lips. She studied her father's face—anticipation, excitement, adventure.

"Emma, are you listening? Plural marriage is the only way to a celestial exaltation. The Mormon Church is wrong for abandoning it, no matter what the government threatened ... and they lost the priesthood keys, their very authority from heaven, when they accepted the Black race into the priesthood. A man named Partridge now holds all the keys of heavenly authority and he is the *only* man on earth that can solemnize marriage. Do you realize that all other marriages are adulterous. And ... from now on, we'll pay our ten percent tithing to Partridge."

Emma could not believe what she was hearing. Keith sat still and silent.

"You will soon have two mothers and we will be moving to a community owned by the priesthood of God—where everyone believes and lives this law."

Stunned, Emma stared at the mother she adored—long auburn hear swept back, high cheek bones, flawless skin, a vivacious women in her early forties with the figure and mannerisms of a women in her twenties. *She's fun, the prettiest mother in the whole neighborhood, she's faithful, an excellent housekeeper, the best cook; why, she's the most perfect mother in the whole world. And Dad is going to replace her?*

She heard her father say, "We studied and prayed and this is what God wants us to do."

"Studied and prayed," Emma whispered under her breath. Fighting tears, she looked at her mother. "Mom, is this what YOU want?"

Forcing a smile, Connie desperately wanted to reassure her children, to convey to them that it would be all right, that somehow all would be well. "Yes ... yes, children," she said quietly.

But Emma knew. Her mother's beautiful and loving heart was shattered. She knew that her mother adored her husband, and that while her own opinions about life often differed from his, she had taken a temple marriage covenant to be faithful to him and obedient to his final decisions because he was the priesthood holder in the family. That is what the Church taught and that is what her mother did.

And what will happen to me? Fighting nausea, her own life flashed before her eyes—*my friends, my plans for the future, my very life.* A stark realization flooded her soul. *My life is over. And Mother? Her life is over, no matter what Dad says.*

Petrified, she dare not say anything. Whatever her dad said was how it would be. There would be no argument. His word was final. That's how she had been brought up.

Emotion surged within her like a raging flood. No longer able to restrain herself, Emma ran to her mother and fell sobbing into her lap.

Chapter Two

Emma's father was a good man, born and raised in the Church. He was the ideal Latter-day Saint with many positive attributes. After serving a successful two-year foreign mission, he came home and quickly married. Before long he held an executive position in a major Utah corporation and provided his wife and children all the luxuries of an upper middle class family.

Connie had been his prize. After his lengthy mission ended, he searched in earnest for the *right* wife, one who was faithful to the Church and all of its teachings, and who would be dedicated to the same goals as he. One who would honor him in his final decisions for the family. But he also wanted a beautiful girl, one with life and spunk. And he found her. In fact she was so spunky, he wondered if she could really settle into a marriage where she would honor him as the final law. After all, they frequently argued and he liked the zest of negotiating their differences. But after marriage, she gave him the respect he was looking for. He felt greatly blessed. That Connie could have no more children following an illness and surgery was a heartache to both of them.

Like many native Utahans, Gene was the second generation of a polygamist. His great grandfather had been a stake president with three wives. In those pioneer days, a stake president was required to have three wives. Gene's great-grandmother had been the third wife.

Great-grandfather was a patriarch in the true sense and a zealot defender of the faith and totally obedient to his priesthood superiors. Gene admired the old pioneer for his tenacity, and the more he learned about the old patriarch, the more proud he became of his pioneer heritage. Gene had inherited many of the noble and stubborn characteristics of this man, who was more concerned with his standing in the Church than his popularity among men.

One Sunday, a group of men in Gene's ward discussed the reasons and role of polygamy during the early days of the Church. Their views were many, the explanations speculative. The popular consensus was that polygamy was adopted because there were more women than men. It wasn't until Gene researched the Church's *Journal of Discourses* that he discovered the official justification for a plurality of wives.

He learned that polygyny, one man with two or more wives, was the order of marriage encouraged and practiced by the early Mormons, not polygamy, which means that either sex can have more than one mate. He studied the discourses of Brigham Young[1] who declared that polygyny was the only conduit to a celestial heavenly exaltation, and it was a commandment to all Latter-day Saints. Gene learned that the *law of celestial marriage* itself had never been repudiated and was still contained in the Mormon law book, Section 132 of the Doctrine and Covenants.

Nearly all the early Mormon Church leaders, Parley P. Pratt, Heber C. Kimball, John Taylor, and a host of others preached that polygyny was a commandment that would never be taken from the earth. Brigham Young also taught that polygyny was introduced to raise up a righteous seed and to prepare men to become kings and priests and rulers of men. And then Gene learned that contemporary fundamentalists like Joseph Musser, who secretly practiced polygyny after the Manifesto, taught that the God of this world was Adam and that a man with the proper priesthood could be the Adam of many worlds, one for each wife. The more wives, the greater his kingdom. The more wives, the greater the man. And then Gene read that Joseph Smith[2] had thirty-three wives, ages 14 to 53, and that Joseph guaranteed the salvation of each wife.[3] And finally, Gene learned that contemporary Mormon fundamentalists believed that in 1886, when Prophet John Taylor was in hiding, he received a revelation that the Church one day would abandon polygamy; so he set apart a group of men to secretly perpetuate plural marriage until the Second Coming of the Savior. The fundamentalists produced all kinds of literature they said supported their position.

One thing lead to another. When Gene attempted to discuss the doctrine of plural marriage with his bishop and stake president, he was not asked, *but told* to leave it alone. That only made him more curious. Eventually he converted to Mormon fundamentalism. And Gene thought he had converted Connie, his wife of eighteen years.

Emma and her father were alone in the car traveling to her first church meeting with polygamists. Her head was still swirling as her father continued to reassure her. It was Priesthood and Girls Class night. While the men and boys attended their meetings, the teenage unmarried girls met in the basement where they were taught not only the *fundamentalist* version of the Mormon gospel, but also the virtues of womanhood. Plural wives from the group aristocracy tutored the girls.

After the opening exercises, the deacons, teachers and priests, all boyhood priesthood positions, would file out to their respective classes where adults instructed them in Mormon fundamentalism. The adults stayed in the auditorium where it was inculcated by a member of the high priest quorum that they, the ruling council, did indeed have the priesthood authority they claimed. Twelve-year-old Keith, a deacon, should have been with his father. But Keith had refused to go.

The meeting place was a two-level square structure made of concrete walls and resembled a warehouse, not a chapel. A baptismal font, kitchen, library, large dining area and classroom were located on the lower level. A stage, auditorium, and eight small classrooms along the western wall comprised the upper level. The auditorium doubled as a basketball court once a week and dance floor once a month.

It was mid April, the evening air cool. The parking lot was half filled with automobiles. Men and boys in long-sleeved shirts and jeans were climbing the stairs to the upper level entrance as teenage girls angled through the parked cars to the lower level entrance.

"I have arranged for a young lady named Mary to show you around," said Gene. "Mary comes from one of the original polygamous families. Her father is on the ruling council."

Emma's eyes darted from person to person as they walked through the parking lot. *They all look normal.* A cluster of talkative girls had gathered outside the east entrance. The girls were attired in either long dresses or skirts and blouses.

Emma had expected the girls to look like the Colorado City polygamous women with the conspicuously wavy hairdos. She was glad to be wrong.

Inside, girls were milling around, chatting in groups of three and four. No one seemed to notice Emma, which suited her just fine. A plain looking girl broke away from two other girls and approached with her hand extended.

"This is Mary," her dad said. "She'll show you around. I'll meet you here after priesthood." And then he disappeared up the stairs. Emma felt abandoned in a strange world.

Mary wore no makeup. Her long dusty blonde hair was combed back and fixed in a pony tail. The blue cotton dress hanging loosely from her shoulders was obviously hand sewn. She looked the same age as Emma, but was ordinary in every respect. Emma thought that with a little makeup and proper clothes she would be a pretty girl.

"Come on," said Mary happily, "I'll introduce you to a couple of my friends." Emma nodded with no other choice but to make the most of an awkward situation.

Emma was led to two girls standing off by themselves. One was of the same bland mold as Mary except with an aura of authority. She was the taller of the two and appeared to be lecturing the other girl, a full bosomed brunette with short hair. Gesturing towards the brunette, Mary said, "Gwen, this is Emma. Her parents are new to the group."

Gwen's warm smile exposed white evenly spaced teeth. Her brown eyes sparkled. She was slightly overweight but on her it looked good. Like Emma, she was wearing a skirt and blouse open at the throat; although the blouse was modest, it complemented her large, well-formed bosoms.

"Welcome to the inner sanctum," Gwen said sarcastically. "I know just what you are going through. My folks joined the group two years ago." Emma immediately liked Gwen.

Turning towards the other girl, Mary said, "This is Claudia."

Claudia's blue eyes narrowed as she looked Emma up and down. "Hummmm," she muttered and then without saying hello, welcome, or go to hell, said "well, I got to go," turned and left.

Emma watched her swagger away.

Gwen chuckled. "Don't mind her, she's a blue blood and blue-blooded kids are always cool to new converts."

"Why … what do you mean?" asked Emma.

"You'll find that kids in the group are more cliquish than other kids," said Gwen. "Claudia comes from an elite family, one of the aristocrats. The blue bloods think we should all bow down to them because of who they are." Gwen chuckled contemptuously. "They think they are the only ones who have ever sacrificed for their religion. My dad lost his job when he took another wife and joined the group. Now he works at a job he hates and it only pays half the money he used to make. All our relatives have disowned us. But the blue bloods don't think that's sacrificing. To put it bluntly," Gwen said with a mischievous twinkle, "they think they are better than the rest of us."

Emma looked at Mary. "You're not snooty and my dad said you come from one of the original families."

Gwen answered for Mary. "That's because there is a pecking order even among the elite families. Mary's mother is a second-class wife." Gwen quickly turned to Mary. "You know what I mean." Mary nodded agreement. "Mary's mother isn't really a second-class wife. Mary knows I didn't mean any disrespect. Her mother's the best mother in their family and one of the best women in the whole group. She's just not the favorite wife, so her children are treated the same way, as inferior children."

"I guess that means I'm a second-class polygamist kid," said Emma.

"That's right," answered Gwen. "Especially if you use eye shadow and lipstick."

"But you've got makeup on," noticed Emma.

"You're darn right, and I intend to keep using makeup," said Gwen saucily. "When you walked up, self-righteous Claudia was chewing me out because I wear makeup and open my blouse at the neck. She's not fooling me. She's just jealous because the boys look at me and not her."

"It's not just the boys that look at you," interjected Mary. "You need to be careful."

Gwen laughed. Looking at Emma, she said, "I'm keeping

score. So far I've had five married men tell me they received a revelation that God wants me to be their plural wife."

Seeing Emma's alarm, Gwen giggled and went on, "It happens all the time. At first it kind of scared me but now we all laugh about it. These guys think we're dumb and can't see through their phony revelations." She leaned closer to Emma and whispered, "We call it penis revelation."

Emma was stunned.

"You're a pretty girl and new to the group," said Gwen. "I'll bet within three months some pious stud in his twenties or thirties corners you at the dance and pulls the revelation gag."

"What do you tell them!" asked Emma, trying to maintain her composure.

"I tell them if and when God gives me the same revelation then *maybe* I'll consider their proposal."

Mary said, "I had one guy tell me that revelations about marriage matches only come through the priesthood. I told him I'd still have to pray about it."

Just then a stout lady in her thirties called from the classroom door. "It's time girls. Let's get started."

Mary, Gwen, and Emma sat together in the back. Emma studied the lady in charge, her name was Barbara.

She wore a brown skirt, tan blouse with sleeves reaching to the wrists, and a charcoal-brown vest. Her diction was letter perfect and she spoke with confidence and matriarchal authority. Barbara was obviously an intelligent woman.

Gwen nudged Emma and whispered, "Barbara is a legal secretary. See how she rolls up her garments so she can wear regular dresses."

Emma peered over the shoulders of the other girls. Just below the hem of Barbara's skirt, tucked inside nylon stockings, she could see the temple garment.

"I can't see any difference between rolling up the garment legs and cutting the legs off," said Gwen sarcastically. "The undergarment is *supposed* to protect the body. The people in this group worship the garment. They say to take it off or mutilate it is a greater sin than adultery. But because Barbara is such a grand lady she's permitted to roll her garments up so she can make lots of money and give it to her husband."

"I get the distinct impression you don't care for the group," Emma whispered back.

"That's right and I'm not alone. Most of the kids raised in the group can't wait to get out. It's so unfair. The elite families get all the breaks. The rest of us are supposed to be happy with crumbs."

Claudia, seated two rows ahead, turned and stared daggers at Gwen and Emma. Gwen wrinkled her nose back at Claudia. "That's her way of telling us to keep quiet," Gwen whispered.

The lesson delivered by Barbara dealt with virtue, chastity, and obedience to priesthood. Overall, Emma thought it was a good lesson and in all fairness, she was impressed with Barbara's sincerity. Barbara obviously believed everything she taught.

Emma knew she must try hard to be open to this new life her father said was essential to her salvation. She even prayed and asked God for help with her poor attitude, something her mother said she had done. But her internal war would not subside.

Barbara stated that Brother Partridge and the priesthood council were infallible and their priesthood edicts were not to be questioned. She told the class that God would not allow the priesthood to lead them astray. Obedience to priesthood was tantamount to obedience to God. To rebel against the priesthood, Barbara said, was the same as rebelling against God.

As Emma listened to Barbara, she knew that this teaching was no different from her traditional Mormon upbringing. Her only question was, does the Partridge group really hold the priesthood keys, or not, because she had been taught her whole life that the Mormon Church held the only keys of heavenly authority to act in God's name.

Emma leaned over to Gwen and whispered, "How is this teaching any different from what we've been taught in the Mormon Church?"

"Oh ..." she said to Emma. "They want you to let the priesthood do ALL your thinking for you. Then when Brother Partridge or some other man on the council tells you to marry so-and-so, you won't question his judgement."

"You mean they tell you who to marry!"

"Not always, but it does happen," Gwen replied, "Mary's

father is trying to get her to marry the son of an elite family. He says it will create an important bond between the two families. She's not ready to marry and besides, even if she were, she doesn't want this guy. So she keeps putting him off. Her father is an apostle and is more concerned with his own standing in the group than he is with her happiness."

"That's awful," whispered Emma.

"I know." Gwen pulled Emma closer, "How caught up are you in the group? I mean, do you buy this polygamy stuff?"

"Heavens no." Emma replied, embarrassed to reveal to this new friend her serious consideration of polygamy. "I'm only here because of my mother and dad."

"That's what I thought," said Gwen. "Mary doesn't buy it either and she was born in the group. As soon as we get the chance, we're gone. Do you want to go with us?"

"Well … sure… I guess … but what about your families?"

Gwen shrugged, "So, do you want your freedom, or not?"

As the meeting was about to come to a close, Claudia raised her hand.

"Yes, Claudia," said Barbara.

"We have a new girl in class."

"Thank you, Claudia," said Barbara. "And where is she?"

"In the back with Mary and Gwen." Emma wanted to crawl under her chair.

"Would you stand please, and introduce yourself?" asked Barbara. The whole class turned to face Emma.

Face flushing, she stood up. "My name is Emma and … uh … and my parents just joined the group." Seeing the amusement on Claudia's face, Emma wasn't about to let the girl enjoy her embarrassment. So she finished with gusto, "I'm so very happy to be here and really looking forward to meeting all of you."

"Thank you," said Barbara sincerely. "We're delighted to have you. This Saturday night is our monthly dance. We hope you will come."

Claudia was asked to say the closing prayer. Emma listened carefully. It seemed to be more of a eulogy to Richard Partridge and the priesthood than to deity.

It was late when Emma and her dad returned home. She had said little during the drive as her father inquired how her evening went. Meeting the other teenagers and hearing their various attitudes about polygamy only reinforced her doubts and fears. She had expected to meet girls who were firmly committed to polygamy, girls she could like and admire. She had desperately needed that lifeline. And so far the only girls she met who seemed to believe in polygamy, she didn't like.

All her lifelong friends were for all practical purposes gone, they would never understand what her family had done. She needed new friends to replace the old, girls she could bear her soul to and unload all that she was feeling. Only then could she get some perspective. But after tonight, she could see there was no one, no one but God.

A spiritual girl, she wanted to do whatever God said was important. Since childhood, she had been taught to listen carefully to what was taught at church, and then to pray about it and get her own personal witness that it was true. But Emma had always questioned her ability to get an answer she could understand. Her concern was, "have I received an answer or not … maybe I only think I have." How do I really know. And then there were the times she didn't really want an answer, because then she would be committed to following it. And this was her problem now.

This polygamy thing was so life changing, her entire belief system was in chaos. She desperately wanted to keep her childlike faith in her father, to believe that he would always keep his family safe. Her parents had appeared to always agree on major decisions. But never before had a decision so devastated her mother. Never before had Emma had to choose between her love for her mother and her loyalty to her father.

Exhausted from the evening, Emma knelt beside her bed and pleaded in earnest that Heavenly Father give her that heartfelt feeling that this was where her family was supposed to be. Finally she fell into bed, heaved a giant sigh, and was immediately asleep.

Chapter Three

Balloons were duct taped to the concrete walls. At the foot of the stage a cassette player attached to the public address system played music. A curly-haired man dressed in a long-sleeved cowboy shirt and blue jeans tapped his foot to the "Tennessee Waltz" while thirty lively couples waltzed enthusiastically up and down the floor. The length of two walls were lined with folding chairs. About twenty people, mostly shy or gossiping teenagers, sat in the chairs chatting or watching the dancers. Gwen led Emma to a space of eight empty chairs.

"I'm really glad you decided to come. You never know, sometimes you can actually have fun at these dances. Besides, you need to see for yourself what they're like."

"I hope I'm not going to regret this," Emma replied nervously. "I keep feeling like some old man is going to walk up and propose to me."

Gwen laughed. "Not hardly. The proper procedure is for the man to approach the father of the proposed bride and ask permission, first to court and second to marry."

Just then Mary appeared and sat down. With Mary was Sally, a younger sister, age fourteen. After they all said 'hi,' Mary sniffed the air and asked Gwen, "What's that you're wearing? It smells good."

"Tommy Girl," answered Gwen and reached into her purse. She handed Mary a small bottle. Mary said, "Thanks," then peeked in both directions before dabbing a drop on her neck under each ear. Mary looked at Emma, "My father won't let any of us girls wear makeup, perfume or earrings. So I sneak it from Gwen. Do you think I'm a sinner?"

"Heavens no," answered Emma.

"I used to feel guilty," said Mary, "but I don't any more. Sometimes when I go to the mall with Gwen I put lipstick on, but I have to scrub it off before going home."

Emma glanced at Mary's hands. Her fingernails were clean but lacked polish. In contrast, Gwen's nails were painted turquoise. Emma had feared she would have to go without makeup or fingernail polish and was grateful to see there was a choice.

Just then a tall, lanky boy in a red and black cowboy shirt dropped in the seat next to Gwen. "Hello, Nephi," Gwen said.

"Gwen," the boy said indignantly, "how many times have I told you not to call me Nephi?"

"I'm sorry … Bruce," Gwen said mischievously.

Bruce looked at Emma hoping for a little sympathy. "I hate the name Nephi," he said. "Gwen loves to tease me about it." And then an expression appeared on Bruce's face like he was about to bawl. "Why would any parent want to name their kid Nephi? How could a parent do that to their own kid?"

She liked this lanky, naive youth, even if his teeth were crooked and he had an Adam's apple like Ichabod Crane.

"Why don't you like the name Nephi?" Emma asked.

"Because it's so churchy and Mormon. How many other guys do you know with the name Nephi. None, I'll bet."

"I was named after Emma Smith, Joseph's first wife," Emma volunteered. "But I don't mind because … you know … Emma was against polygamy." Emma inwardly cringed in her need to be accepted by this group of kids.

Realizing that Emma and Bruce had not met, Gwen made the introductions and Bruce stuck out his hand eager to shake Emma's hand. His palm was rough and callused. Impulsively she said, "Your skin is so rough."

His face flushed. "I'm sorry. I guess I should of put lotion on them. It's just that I don't like to wear gloves."

"What kind of work do you do?" she asked.

"I'm a contractor," he replied with unfeigned pride. "I build houses."

"Who do you work for?" asked Emma.

"I'm a general contractor," he said with a hint of arrogance. "I work for myself."

"Well, I'm impressed," answered Emma. "I would never have guessed. You're so young. How old are you?"

"I'll be twenty next month," he said, puffing out his chest.

Gwen interrupted. "Bruce, tell Emma why you started up your own business."

Bruce looked at Gwen, then at Emma. "Well, I wanted to be my own boss."

"Bruce," Gwen said impatiently, "tell Emma why you wanted to be your own boss or I'll start calling you Nephi again."

He flashed Gwen a weary look. Then he said almost timidly, "I use to work for my brother … that is, my half-brother. We have the same dad but different moms. He and some other men in the group formed a company and started building big apartment complexes. That's where I learned to be a framer."

"What's a framer?" asked Emma.

"A framer is the guy who frames the structure. You know, the walls, roof, windows."

Bruce went on to tell how his half-brother and the others hired young men from the group to do the work, but they paid them less than union scale wages because "we were doing God's work and should be glad to have the job." But men hired from outside the group were paid the standard wage. It was totally unfair.

"That's when I decided to go into business for myself," said Bruce. "Some of the others did the same thing. I took some carpentry classes at Trade Tech, got my contractor's license and found a builder that gave me a chance. He liked the first house I built and now he's given me five more."

"But you're so young," said Emma.

"That's what others say, but I don't think so. I've been building houses since I was fourteen. I've proved myself. Now I'm on my own and the priesthood isn't going to get another cent out of me." He hesitated and took a double look at Emma. "Do you think I'm wicked?" he asked.

"Not at all," she replied. "I think you're very mature and smart not to give your money away." He beamed with delight.

A man in his early twenties asked Gwen to dance. As Emma watched the man lead Gwen to the floor, Bruce said clumsily, "Would you like to dance?"

She couldn't turn him down. She had never met a more sincere, polite young man, but dancing with Bruce was like dancing with a stiff board.

26

They had no sooner returned to their seats when Emma was approached by a handsome man in his early thirties. Emma was scared to death. But he was polite, charming, and insistent. His demeanor implied that she should be flattered.

"My name is Seth and I would like to welcome you to the group."

"I'm not a very good dancer," she said, hoping it would discourage him. He wore a powder blue sport shirt under a navy blue blazer. The shirt matched his blue eyes. Seth was suave, unlike Bruce and the other men who were more country and unpretentious. Seth's tan slacks and expensive loafers were in sharp contrast to the blue jeans and cowboy boots of the other men.

"I saw you dancing with Nephi, you were doing fine," he replied.

"You mean Bruce," she corrected.

He shot a feigned apologetic glance at Bruce, "That's right, I forgot," he said insincerely. Then concentrating on Emma, he said, "I'm told your name is Emma, that's a pretty name."

How does he know my name?

"We better hurry before the music stops," he urged, flashing his most charming smile, and pulled her to the dance floor.

The pleasant odor of aftershave lotion was strong. He attempted to pull her close but she resisted. He smiled and tried again. Emma resisted again. She felt like a package of meat being carefully considered.

Seth asked, "How do you like the people in the group?"

"They're okay," she answered indifferently.

"What kind of work do you do?" she asked.

"Oil exploration," he replied.

Emma was grateful to know he was a businessman like her father. "And where do you explore?"

"All through the United States," he said. "There's lots of oil still left to be discovered. But let's talk about you. Do you have a testimony of celestial marriage?"

"You mean plural marriage?"

"Yes." He beamed down at her with an ingratiating grin.

"I ... I guess," Emma replied. "I'm new to the group."

The grin vanished. "But don't you believe in Joseph Smith?"

Suddenly angry at the test he was administering, she answered, "Who's he?"

The leering grin reappeared, "You're just putting me on."

"Am I?" she said.

Seth hesitated, studying her. "I like you," he said excitedly. "You got pluck."

The music stopped and the curly-haired man by the piano yelled, "Everybody pair off for a square dance."

"I only got half a dance," Seth moaned. "Will you square dance with me?"

When the square dance was over, Seth asked Emma for a third dance. She politely told him no.

Back in her chair, Emma asked Mary if she knew how many wives Seth had.

"He has four," Mary said. "And he's looking for a fifth."

Mary and Emma watched as Seth sat with three young women on the other side of the dance floor.

"Are those his wives?" asked Emma.

"Yes," Mary said. "The one in the yellow dress is my cousin."

"They're ... so young," said Emma.

"He likes them young," answered Mary. "My cousin is the youngest, she just turned eighteen."

Emma scrutinized the group. The girl sitting next to Seth looked very pregnant. All three girls appeared to be well mannered, content, and they portrayed the epitome of polygamous bliss. Emma shuddered. *They look like a harem.*

Mary volunteered, "If one of Seth's wives suddenly becomes friendly, look out, that means he wants you."

Just then Emma noticed her father step onto the dance floor. He held the hand of a girl with long blonde hair—and young. *Oh, my God.* She gulped air and her stomach heaved. She knew this day would eventually come, the day she would see her father with another woman.

She immediately hated her father. Fighting to regain composure, she leaned close to Mary and said as calmly as she could, "Who is the blonde lady dancing with my dad?"

"That's Colleen," said Mary, feeling Emma's stress. Mary

didn't volunteer more information, she didn't want to add to Emma's anxiety.

"What can you tell me about her?" Emma asked.

Mary squirmed, gathering her thoughts, wondering how she should break the news. She was surprised Emma didn't already know.

Mary's hesitance alarmed Emma. She took Mary by the arm and squeezed. "Mary, is that lady my father's wife?"

Bruce, returning from the dance floor, sat next to Emma. Right away Bruce sensed that something traumatic was occurring. In spite of his discomfort, he forced himself to stay seated in case he was needed.

"No, at least not yet," replied Mary sympathetically. "I think … I heard they are to be sealed next Sunday after meeting."

Stunned, watching him pull the lady close, both radiating happiness, Emma whispered, "Tell me about her."

"When Colleen was younger," began Mary, "she didn't want anything to do with polygamy. As soon as she turned eighteen, she married someone outside the group, but it didn't work. I heard he smoked pot and abused her, so Colleen divorced him and came back. She said she would rather share a good man with other women than have all of a bad man to herself … I think Colleen really wants to do what is right."

"How did he meet her?"

Mary looked sheepish. But she had to be truthful.

"Colleen's father is on the council and has a lot of influence. He thinks your dad will be a great asset to the group. He arranged for them to meet."

Arranged for them to meet! An arranged marriage?

"What do you mean!"

Mary took a deep breath and looked Emma square in the eyes, "Some people say that Colleen's dad offered her as inducement for your dad to come into the group."

Emma's mouth dropped and she turned to stare at her father, Colleen tight against him, smiling and patting his cheek. Emma turned away, her face white. "Is there more?" she asked Mary.

"Colleen has a baby girl."

"How old is Colleen now?" asked Emma, fighting to retain her composure. Bruce, who now knew what the problem was, looked on compassionately.

"Twenty."

"My dad is more than twenty years older than her."

"That's not uncommon. And sometimes," said Mary, "not so much in our group, but in others, girls marry at fourteen … see, that's what Utah law allows."

The music stopped. A young man brought Gwen back to her chair. Emma was fighting tears.

"What's wrong!" asked Gwen, taking Emma by the arm.

"I want to go home," cried Emma. "I've got to get out of here."

Gwen turned to Mary. "What happened?"

Mary gestured towards the dance floor. "It's her dad."

Gene and Colleen were standing in the middle of the dance floor, still embracing, while the other dancers drifted off the floor. Gwen understood. She signaled Bruce, "Take us home."

Chapter Four

Emma sobbed all the way home. "I hate my dad," she said over and over.

"Don't be too hard on him," said Gwen. "He's just behaving like most other men in the group."

Emma hiccupped and said. "I thought my dad was above … the sex thing."

For one of the few times in her life, Gwen didn't know what to say.

"I HATE him for what he's doing to my mother. And I HATE him for ruining my life."

Finally she had said it.

Bruce pulled in the driveway of Emma's house. The three sat in the car giving Emma a chance to get hold of herself. "Have you told your mother how you feel?" asked Gwen.

"No," sobbed Emma.

"Talk to her," said Gwen. "You can't keep holding all this inside you."

"I don't know," said Emma. "I can't bear to hurt her."

"She's already hurt," said Gwen. "Emma, I went through the same thing. Your mother needs to know how you feel and you need to know how she feels, so talk to her. Promise me."

Emma gave Gwen a hug. "Okay," she said. "I promise."

Connie was in the family room reading a Herman Wouk novel, *The Winds of War*. All the lights were out except for the dim lamp by the chair where her mother was curled up.

"How was the dance?"

"It was okay … I guess," said Emma. "Mom, can we … can we talk?"

"Sure, honey," said Connie. "What about?"

"Mom ... I saw Daddy ... at the dance ... and ... and ..."
Weeks of pent-up emotion erupted. Emma found herself sobbing
in her mother's lap again. "How could he do this to you?" she
repeated over and over.

Connie stroked her daughter's hair as tears trickled down her
own cheeks. Gene had told her he was taking Colleen to the dance
as he half-heartedly invited her also, but Connie knew he would
prefer to go alone. And she was still uncomfortable in Colleen's
presence. Connie had been warned by other women in the group
that once Colleen entered the family, it would be a struggle. But
they reassured her that her reward would come, that she would
gain a higher place in heaven by overcoming jealousy and the other
debilitating emotions triggered by a plural marriage. So far Connie
wasn't doing very well.

An older, wiser matriarch in the group told Connie that the
ideal and less traumatic method of obtaining a sister-wife was for
the first wife to recruit the candidate. But in Colleen's case, her
father said he had been inspired by God to bring them together.
How could you argue with God and the priesthood? But Connie
was finding out that nearly all the decisions of the council were
somehow predicated upon "revelation" from God, who, it
seemed, was much more vocal among the polygamists than he was
in the traditional Mormon Church.

Twenty minutes passed before Emma was able to stop crying,
then she poured out her feelings, describing the sickness she felt
when she saw her father with another woman. Then she was
exhausted.

"Mom," Emma pleaded. "I've got to know what you're
thinking ... how you feel."

Connie raised Emma's head, kissed her check, and wiped
away the tears. She chose her words carefully.

Emma looked up at her mother's face. She thought it was
never more beautiful—for the first time in weeks, her mother was
once again relaxed, a fountain of wisdom, confident, and
overflowing with love. Auburn curls hung loosely around her ears
and forehead.

"My first priority," Connie said softly, "is to keep the family
together ... at all costs."

"Even over your own feelings?" asked Emma.

"Especially over my own feelings," she replied. "I have to think what's best for you and Keith."

"Don't worry about me, Mom, I just want you to be happy. I don't want you to be hurt. But if Daddy marries Colleen …who's only three years older than me … I don't think I can keep from hating them both."

"Don't blame Colleen," said Connie. "Colleen is really a nice girl. She's only trying to find some security and happiness in life."

"But at your expense," interjected Emma.

"Well, yes and no. In Colleen's mind she's not taking your father away from me, she's sharing him. This is the way she was brought up. She tried a monogamous marriage and it didn't work."

"Daddy's old enough to be her father," Emma said spitefully.

"I know, but Colleen is looking for stability and security. The age difference they can overcome … at least for the moment. What it will be like when your dad is in his seventies, only time will tell. But from Colleen's point of view, your dad's a good catch. He'll be good to her."

"And what about your security, Mom?"

Emma brushed the hair out of her eyes, sat on the floor, and pulled her knees up under her chin.

"I'm dealing with it, darling," said Connie. "I have to admit, I don't feel very secure right now, but I'm dealing with it the best I can."

"Mom, I don't want to live polygamy. I can't get an answer from Heavenly Father. Do you really believe you're supposed to live it … I mean really?"

Connie pondered Emma's question. She had asked herself that same question a hundred times … and she still wasn't sure.

"You know," Connie said, "I don't know why I haven't talked to you about this before. Good heavens, you're grown up and it won't be long till you'll be getting married and starting a family of your own. You have every right to know what your dad and I are thinking. The only reason we haven't discussed it with you more is that we didn't think you would understand, and we wanted to spare you any more distress."

"I know, Mom, but I'm glad we're talking now."

"So am I and I'm going to be perfectly honest." Connie gave a big sigh. "I don't have a testimony of plural marriage either. I have prayed about it and nothing happens, no burning of the bosom or emotional uplift like I've always been taught to look for if the heavens are speaking to me. I was brought up to believe that Joseph Smith was a prophet and he said plural marriage was correct. If I accept Joseph Smith, I guess I have to accept plural marriage. Besides, your father is absolutely convinced plural marriage must be lived now, by him … so I went along to save the family. I guess I was afraid he would leave us if I didn't. Other men have.

"Emma, the commandment for plural marriage has never been repudiated. It still exists in the 132nd Section of the Doctrine & Covenants. I understand why the Church discontinued the practice; after all, the government forced them. But because the doctrine is still listed in Mormon scriptures, the polygamists make a good case. Of course, Mormons today interpret it as a doctrine that will apply to their lives in heaven, not here."

"Well," said Emma, "I don't care how good a case they make, deep in my heart I don't want anything to do with plural marriage and Mom, I'm finding out lots of kids in the group feel the same way."

"Then you've made some friends?" asked her mother. "I'm glad."

"There's this girl Gwen. She's not afraid to say what she thinks. I really like her. Her family came into the group about two years ago so she knows exactly how I feel. And then there's Mary. She was born in the group but her mother is a second-class mother …" Emma glanced at her mother, "I mean, she's not the favorite wife. Anyway, Mary doesn't like polygamy either because of the way she and her mother are treated by the elite families. Mom, the kids in the group are more cliquish than even the kids in school or in our old ward. Some are really conceited, and others are super nice. The real nice ones are those who are getting out of the group the first chance they get."

"I've noticed the superior attitude among the adults," said Connie. "As for me, I've been treated well by everyone. But … it didn't take me long to pick out the inferior families from the elite families."

"Mary told me Colleen's father thinks Daddy is going to be a great asset to the group and that's why he arranged for Colleen to marry him."

"I knew that," Connie sighed. "The priesthood leaders are going out of their way to make your dad welcome. And the leading women, the wives with the most power and influence, are going out of their way to make me feel welcome. I don't know if I should be flattered or on guard."

"What are we going to do, Mom?"

"Well," said Connie, "I promised your father I would give it a chance. I will keep that promise. Let's just take it a day at a time, okay. And no more crying or worrying about me. Promise."

"Promise," said Emma and gave her mother a big hug.

John R. Llewellyn

Chapter Five

Sunday arrived and Emma's father would wed his first plural wife. Connie's Friday night sleep was labored, Saturday night she didn't sleep at all. When she climbed out of bed Sunday morning, bags hung under weary eyes.

Outside, it was still dark. A few cumulus clouds had boiled up over the Great Salt Lake. The wind was from the northwest, mild but humid.

It wasn't a typical Sunday. Today Connie would give to her husband a plural wife. That's how it worked, the first wife gives to her husband the second wife, just like Sarah gave Leah to Abraham.

The marriage ceremony is a sacred and important ritual in the Mormon religion. The temples were built first for the endowment, where an individual makes formal and eternal covenants with God, and then for the important marriage ceremony.

The Partridge group didn't have a temple—yet. But it did have a structure where endowments, prayer circles, and marriages were conducted. Obscured by an innocent looking door on the second floor that presumed to open up a closet was actually the secret holy of holies where only the prophet Partridge and his most loyal advisors were permitted. A pillowed white alter was attached to an oak wood floor with a large Star of David engraved in the center. Two mock vertical-fluted pillars were situated on either side of the alter. Gossamer curtains in soft shades of pink, white, and blue covered the walls. In this holy of holies the Savior was supposed to someday appear and give instruction to the prophet, who would be patiently waiting. On special occasions, prayer circles were held there by the most righteous and worthy members of the group. In the prayer circles the sick were blessed, men were praised or cursed.

In the basement of the building the symbolic washing and

anointing ordinance was performed and the long sacred undergarment was placed on the initiate. The sleeves of the garment came down to the wrists, the legs to the ankles, it had a collar that opened in front and was held together by a series of three strings tied in bows.

"What is that you're wearing, Mother?" a sleepy Emma asked, looking her mother up and down. It looked very uncomfortable. And then she remembered that Gwen had called her attention to Barbara's rolled up garment in girls class.

"This is the *original* temple garment," Connie explained and pointed at several symbols sewn into the garment. "The collar," she said, "represents the yoke of Christ that we take upon ourselves. The Mormon Church has shortened the garment and removed the yoke to accommodate the fashions of today. What you see me wearing is the original pattern revealed to Joseph Smith." The tone of Connie's voice suggested she was discussing a very sacred topic.

Connie slipped panties on over the garment and then a bra.

Mom, I love you, but you look ridiculous.

"But Mom, why are you doing another endowment. You already did that when you got married, didn't you?" Connie's face looked strained, so Emma dropped the subject.

At 5:00 a.m. her parents left for the endowment house. Children were not invited. Connie said they would be back in time for Sunday School.

Emma went back to bed and stared at the ceiling, restless and nervous, angry that her life had turned upside down. She thrashed around in the bed trying to get comfortable. Suddenly panic grabbed her.

Something is wrong! She sat up on the edge of the bed. *Why am I such a wreck?*

It's Mom! Emma could *feel* that her mother was ill.

At that very moment, in the Celestial Room of the endowment house, kneeling before the pillowed alter, Connie, fighting nausea, was giving Colleen to be her husband's plural wife.

Tears threatening, Emma shook off the feeling, showered, dressed for Sunday School and was nibbling at a bowl of cereal when Connie walked in the front door—alone. She looked exhausted. Keith was still in the bathroom.

"Where's Dad?" Emma asked.

"He's with Colleen."

"How come? The wedding isn't until tonight."

"Well," Connie said, choosing her words carefully. "Actually, the marriage took place this morning."

"What do you mean?" Emma demanded.

"I didn't want you to worry about me, Emma, and I knew you would. The marriage this afternoon is only a re-enactment for you children and others who were not worthy to attend the ceremony in the endowment house." Connie dropped into a kitchen chair.

Emma studied her mother. Empathy overcame her anger. Her mother was tired. She didn't need any more stress. She had just been through a terrible ordeal, giving her husband to another woman. And she was supposed to be overjoyed about it. *What a crock.*

"But why put you through this again?" said Emma, raising her voice. "Isn't once enough?" She stood up in disgust and stomped around the kitchen. "I think it's sick!"

"Emma, sit down for a minute," her mother pleaded softly. "It happens in the Mormon Church also. Not everybody can get a temple recommend. So to satisfy non-members and those who are unable to get a temple recommend, some people hold both a temple wedding and a civil wedding. This is no different."

"Well, I'm not going."

"If you don't go, it will cause feelings," said Connie. "Your dad will be disappointed and it will create tension between you and Colleen. Besides darling, I need your strength. I don't know if I can do this again."

Connie went back to bed. She fell into exhausted sleep mixed with foreboding and visions of Colleen escorting an army of cousins, aunts, and girlfriends to wed Gene, lined up as far as the eye could see. And suddenly she saw another line with Emma, standing zombie-like with other girls, waiting her turn to be married to an old man with a grin. Unruly gray hair hung down to his shoulders, his clothes homespun like a pioneer. Connie shot up out of bed in a cold sweat.

They stayed home from Sunday School. Keith didn't complain because he didn't get along with the other polygamist kids. Even the boys were cliquish, slow and cautious in making friends. So at his new public school, he made friends with non-polygamist kids, and seeing him with the *gentiles*, the polygamist boys wrote him off. But Keith didn't care.

Because Keith was a boy, and the youngest, and always preoccupied with sports, his feelings towards polygamy were unintentionally neglected. In reality, he was having a more difficult time coping than Emma, but because of his tender years he did not know how to express his frustration. So he kept it inside. Scolded by his father when he refused to go to priesthood, Keith became sullenly silent.

It wasn't that Keith was physically afraid of the other boys. He was ready to fight if necessary. It was the shunning, the whispering, the "I'm better than you smugness" that he couldn't stand. He was not about to grovel. It only took two unpleasant meetings to turn Keith against the principle. Once his negative attitude took root it was immovable. He yearned deeply for his old friends.

Connie fixed ham sandwiches for lunch. It would soon be time to leave for sacrament meeting, but Emma didn't want to go. Neither did Keith. Their mother persisted. "Children, we have to keep up appearances." Emma didn't know if she could bear to watch her mother struggle through another ridiculous ceremony.

"By the way," Connie said, breaking the negative mood, "I think I've found a job."

Both Keith and Emma stared at their mother.

"What job?" asked Keith. "Why you gotta get a job?"

"Well, Keith," she replied. "We will need the money. Your dad is going to have two families now, so there won't be as much money to go around. Besides, most of his money is going toward building our new house." She looked at Emma. "And there's another reason … it will help occupy my mind."

"Where you go'n to work, Mom," asked Keith, "some place neat like Burger King?"

"No," she answered with a smile. "At a real estate office. I might even get my own license."

"Cool," said Emma. "When do you start?"

"A week from tomorrow. I want this week free so the three of us can do a few things together before I start work."

Yes, and it will help take your mind off Dad and Colleen doing "it" on their honeymoon.

"What are we gonna do?" asked Keith.

"Go to movies, hike, visit museums, fish, the zoo, anything you want, as long as we have fun."

"Can we go to a baseball game?"

"You bet," replied Connie. "I'd love to see a baseball game."

It was important to Gene and Colleen that while at sacrament meeting they look just like the other polygamous families. That meant they all must file in together and sit together. Gene and Colleen were waiting in the parking lot when Connie and the kids pulled up, all dressed in their Sunday finery.

Gene led the way through the parking lot and Colleen followed, with Connie, Emma, and Keith bringing up the rear. The parking lot and entrance was a swirl of moving bodies with smiling faces, that special church smile that automatically appears on all Mormons within fifty yards of the chapel.

It was a scene to behold. The uplifted corners of the mouth and sparkle in the eyes, fixed in perpetual greeting, never faltering, regardless of the rhetoric. The jealousies, family fights, poverty, power struggles, political conspiracies, social inadequacies, priesthood ambitions, and self doubts, all masked over by the perfunctory grins; and at the end of the session the men would slap on each other's back and rave about what a wonderful meeting it had been, giving that contented "I've been spiritually fed" look. For they were a hardy optimistic bunch, committed and determined to make sacrament meeting a pleasant experience.

Once they entered the chapel, Gene halted. He surveyed the rows of chairs looking for five seats together. He took his time, giving those already seated a chance to look him over and see that now he was really one of them. Colleen beamed with delight, knowing they were all on display. She was at home and comfortable in the polygamous element. Connie and Emma felt awkward, but Keith could give a rat's ass. A fellow waving a handkerchief halfway towards the back finally got Gene's attention and motioned that he had saved them seats.

On the stage sat Richard Partridge and ten of his twelve apostles. All wore suits, white shirts, and ties except for Mary's father, who was attired in a checkered cowboy shirt with an arrowhead bolo tie, and another man with a grimy white shirt under a green sweater. The demeanor of the apostolic council was to a man somber and severe, their grievous faces reflecting the great weight of their calling. The men on the stage did their best to portray the role of a unified priesthood *deeply concerned* with the ultimate salvation of those who followed their counsel. Colleen's father was among them and beamed approvingly at Gene. Connie, aware they were being scrutinized, bit her lip. Emma felt like puking. Colleen beamed with delight. Keith pulled out a pack of baseball cards and thumbed through them.

Finally, Brother Partridge stepped to the podium, "Brother and sisters, it's time to start our meeting."

The congregation sang the opening song with usual gusto, using music as an opportunity to express their enthusiasm and commitment to religion.

After the sacrament had been passed, Brother Partridge asked Colleen's dad to conduct the meeting. He rose to the occasion and with a deep baritone voice delivered an eloquent discourse attesting that Richard Partridge held the keys to the kingdom of God and Partridge would not, could not, lead the people astray. He went on for twenty minutes pounding away at the notion that of the billions of people on the earth and the hundreds of thousands of religious sects that claimed authority, the true gospel of God and the only true priesthood was standing before them. As unworthy as the people were, if they would follow the living, true priesthood they would find eternal salvation and become kings and priests and rulers of men. In time, he said, seven women would plead to cling to one man. Soon the days of trepidation would be at hand, he warned, and the holocaust would consume the world. Only where the priesthood of God was centered would the inhabitants of earth be safe. And of course the priesthood was centered there, on the stage. He told the congregation how fortunate they were.

When his discourse finally expired, out of the blue, Colleen's dad called Gene to the stand. Colleen whispered, "Well, look at you! This will help our standing in the group."

Gene was still reeling from the morning events and riding on a spiritual high. He floated to the podium where for ten minutes he praised the group, praised Richard Partridge, and praised his family. After the meeting, everybody patted him on the back and told him what a wonderful job he did.

By the time the closing prayer was called for, Emma was dozing. Colleen's father asked a little dark headed man to say the benediction. Emma was jolted awake when the little man pleaded for God to speed up the destruction of the United States government. She glanced at Richard Partridge, expecting him to correct the man, but Partridge did not. Emma glanced at the people around her. No reaction. She looked at her mother, clearly as bewildered as Emma. After the meeting was over, Emma quickly found Gwen and asked her why the man had prayed for the destruction of the government.

Gwen explained, "They still blame the government for killing Joseph Smith and legally forbidding fundamentalists from living plural marriage."

The wedding ceremony was short and to the point. It was held in the home of Colleen's mother where Colleen's father would again marry Colleen to Gene for time and all eternity. Colleen stood on Gene's left, Connie, as first wife, on his right.

Richard Partridge graced the momentous event with his favorite wife. Two sister-wives of Colleen's mother were also present. It was a small, exclusive crowd devoid of pomp and pretension.

Colleen's father welcomed all in attendance, hesitated, looked at Connie and nodded. It was the signal for Connie to reach around Gene, take Colleen's right hand and place it in Gene's right hand.

Emma could tell by the expression on her father's face that he was struggling with his feelings. When Connie placed Colleen's hand in his, he looked at Connie, his wife of eighteen years, and felt true compassion and genuine love for her. Connie's eyes were downcast and did not meet his, her countenance emotionless, her movements mechanical. He turned back to Colleen. Their eyes met and his face brightened. It was Colleen's time, her big day, and as sorry as he felt for Connie, he could not rob Colleen of her debut. Like hundreds of honorable polygamist men before him, he promised himself some day to make it up to his first wife.

Connie's eyes left the carpet only for a quick glance at Emma, who flashed a supportive smile. Keith, who stood by Emma, was confused, not understanding fully what was going on, but whatever it was, he didn't like it. He didn't like the way Partridge, Colleen's father, and Colleen had disrupted his family.

The deed was done. For the second time that day, Connie had given another woman to her husband for time and for all eternity. From that moment on, her nuptial duty was to share her man and the family assets with another woman, a woman she hardly knew. Emma saw nothing beautiful about the ceremony. Colleen glowed with anticipation, every eye on her … her mother completely ignored.

A deep void had been created in the psyche that was once Connie. She would never be the same. Obedience to a doctrine that demeaned the soul on earth but exalted it in heaven addled her sanity. The only earthly justice to such a system would occur when a third wife came into the family, dethroning the second wife, causing her to experience the same emotional insecurity and deflation.

The introduction of a third wife would automatically redefine the roles of all the wives. The function of the first wife then became political and matriarchal. Depending on her grit and pugnacity, she might become a greater family influence than her husband, even a tyrant actually presiding over and rationing out her husband's affection and material goods to the subsequent wives. Or, at the other end of the spectrum, she might be relegated to the submissive role of an impotent figurehead, avoiding conflict, nurturing her children, and sewing exquisite blankets. If a tyrant, people would fear her, but respect her judgement and seek her council. If the impotent figurehead, her conformity would be admired and her sweetness extolled.

And Emma was irrevocably changed. Her desire to do what her dad said God wanted her to do was gone. The God she knew was loving, kind, compassionate. He could not condone this.

There were no refreshments. No music. No conversation. No pat on the back for Connie.

Connie sidled up to Gene. He held Colleen in his right arm and was entrenched in political conversation with Brother Partridge. Connie kissed him on the cheek and whispered in his ear, "I'll see you when I see you." He nodded.

Connie gathered up Keith and Emma and exited unnoticed by the back door.

Chapter Six

It didn't take Gene long to sell his subdivision house and start building at the polygamist community, a rural area sixty miles south of Salt Lake City. Incorporated as a town in 1997, the community was located on the side of a hill. Incorporation allowed the priesthood to establish its own zoning ordinances for multi-family homes. In three years, the town had doubled in both population and homes, now totaling forty-five. At the current rate of growth, in ten years they would out populate the monogamists in the county.

The town fathers had developed a trailer court near the cabinet shop that was the only actual business in town. Twenty trailer spaces complete with electricity, water, and sewer hookups were situated ten feet apart in a long neat row.

Gene rented one of the trailers for Connie, Emma, and Keith until their new Four-Plex was completed. Colleen continued to live in her mother's home until its completion. Gene spent one night with Connie and the next night with Colleen.

"Why a Four-Plex?" asked Emma. "You only have two wives."

Gene said, "Honey, as long as we're building, we should prepare for the future. Other good women may want to come into the family."

At first Gene thought his Four-Plex would be owned by the priesthood. But when approached by the bishop of his particular Order to sign an occupancy agreement, he found out the town and its property were actually owned by a land trust in the names of Brother Calvin and four of his sons. Calvin was the younger brother of Richard Partridge, the presiding bishop over all the local bishops and their communities within the Partridge group, and as senior apostle, he was next in line to succeed his older brother.

Gene quickly read through the occupancy agreement and signed without asking questions. After all, if you couldn't trust the bishop, who could you trust? The bishop had said, "Signing the occupancy agreement is mandatory for everyone permitted to build on the property. It just means that all the occupants agree to live in harmony with each other." The bishop further explained, "We don't want anyone building on the property that doesn't think and believe as we do." It made sense. Besides, Gene was still bubbling with jubilation over becoming a part of the great cause. That, coupled with the ego enhancing of having more than one wife, especially a young attractive wife, had disarmed his natural wisdom. The successful businessman Gene was experiencing what hundreds of men before him had experienced, a mind-numbing spiritual intoxication. He would have signed anything the bishop placed before him.

The town was also an Order, that is, a form of the United Order that Brigham Young introduced when the Saints reached the Great Basin. Brigham City and the town of Orderville in Kane County are examples of cities founded on the United Order. Of the several Orders in the Partridge group, this one, where Gene had been permitted to build, was the most prestigious.

Each head of family in an Order was required to disclose to his particular bishop and councilors his gross annual income. From that figure, the bishop would first calculate the tithing, and then the Order dues, leaving the occupant, Gene discovered, barely enough for the simple needs of his family. The dues, like tithing, were considered a donation and became the property of the recipient. Disposition of the money, which amounted to thousands of dollars, was determined by the bishop and his councilors, subject of course to the approval of Calvin. It so happened that the bishopric of Gene's Order was comprised of the sons and son-in-law of Calvin.

Calvin, an aged man of ordinary features in his middle seventies, was undoubtedly the most charming man in the group. He literally oozed with unfeigned love. No one dared think anything derogatory or diabolical about him. If the prophet Richard Partridge should die, Calvin, being the senior apostle, would become leader of the entire group.

Because of the taxes the cabinet shop paid to the county, the people in the community thought they merited special consideration and should be immune from public scrutiny. They minded their own business and attempted to stay out of the public eye. Because they were left alone, they felt they had the right to police their own people. So the handling of judicial disputes was administered by the Order theocracy rather than civil law. All power was vested in Calvin who was also the mayor. And no one complained, or dared to complain. As the community continued to grow unmolested, its people succumbed to an illusion of invulnerability.

Emma, along with other polygamist kids, was bused to a school in a town twenty miles south. Because many of the polygamist boys were the stars of the high school basketball team, the polygamist kids were treated with respect. They were considered so righteous by the people in the county, folks went out of their way to protect them. The polygamists also considered themselves the darlings of the group, but Emma was not impressed and kept her distance. She did not feel superior to anyone.

Her friends were Gwen and Mary and they lived in Salt Lake County, an hour away. She didn't trust the other polygamist kids. Because of her bitterness she prejudged them all as brats like Claudia, snooty, pious robot defenders of the priesthood.

Emma concentrated all of her energy on her studies and became a straight-A student. The principal made her the editor of the school newspaper and her fellow students elected her captain of the debate team. The school counselor tried to encourage her to pursue a degree in law after high school, but Emma's desire was for journalism where she could express her thoughts and satisfy the creative impulses that burned inside her.

She looked forward to Girls Class and the dances where she could visit with her special friends, Gwen, Mary, and good old Bruce. They became the nucleus of a clique of their own that grew to fifteen, much to the consternation of Claudia and her blue-blooded friends.

Bruce continued attending priesthood meeting so he could visit with Mary, Gwen, and Emma. When he could, Bruce would furnish the girls transportation. On Saturdays he occasionally took them shopping at the mall where they wandered up and down window shopping, dreaming of a normal, monogamous future. Bruce had not formed a particular infatuation or attempted to single out any of the girls for himself. His motives where strictly platonic. The unifying factor in their exclusive little circle was the mutual abhorrence of the polygamous lifestyle. The parents of the girls trusted Bruce. He was a hard worker, bright, came from a good family, and had a promising future as a general contractor. From appearances, it was assumed Bruce would become a stalwart in the principle and therefore a potentially good husband for blossoming daughters.

Bruce wisely kept his negative thoughts about the priesthood to himself, confiding only in his friends. Bruce's father and most of the other fathers, busy making a living and soothing the emotions of their wives, were unaware of what was going on in the heads of their children.

Ordinarily, rebellious kids in the outside world are drug users. But not among this band of rebels. Like Emma, they were at the top of their class or otherwise excelled in a chosen endeavor like Bruce. The kids who attended public school were at a distinct academic and cultural advantage over the kids, like Mary and her siblings, who were compelled to attend the priesthood-controlled private school of their group.

It was Friday night when Emma received a phone call from Mary. "Something terrible has happened," Mary whispered. "I've got to talk to someone."

"What happened?" Emma urged.

"I can't talk about it over the phone. Can you come to my house … in the morning … I can have Bruce come and get you."

"Sure," replied Emma. What could possibly be wrong with Mary, unless it was the almost forced marriage she had spoken of.

That night Emma brooded over Mary's phone call. She had never heard Mary so depressed and panicky. Emma knew that girls her age have a tendency to be dramatic. But of all her friends, Mary was the most reserved and even tempered.

At 10 a.m. Bruce and Emma pulled into Mary's driveway at the south end of Salt Lake County. It was an older well-kept house in a regular neighborhood, nothing fancy, but neat and clean. The yard was surrounded by a chain link fence. A swing set took up half the back yard, a vegetable garden the other half.

Bruce said he had some finishing work to do on a house and would pick Emma up later. Maybe they could get a hamburger on the way home. He would be glad to buy.

Mary escorted Emma to her bedroom and closed the door. She shared the small bedroom with her younger sister, Sally. They each had a dresser and took turns in front of a mirror set on a small table. Two younger sisters, Pauline age twelve and Cora age nine, shared the adjacent bedroom. George, fifteen, and Joseph, seven, slept in the basement.

The two friends, dressed in blue jeans and blouses, sat on the edge of the bed. Tears trickled out of Mary's blue eyes.

"What is it?" Emma urged. It was her turn to comfort a friend.

"I have to confide in someone." Mary's words were labored, her face contorted. "A few days ago," she began, "I started to walk out my bedroom door, but … but … my dad was blocking the way. When I tried to get past him, he grabbed my T-shirt at the neck and looked down at my breasts." Mary hesitated, waiting for Emma's reaction.

"Did he … did he say anything?" Emma asked, stunned to her soul.

"He said he wanted to see how I was growing. He couldn't see much, I was wearing a bra. I didn't know what to do, I was in shock. Finally I pulled away and went into the kitchen. I didn't leave my mother's side until he left."

"Mary, did … did anything else happen?"

"No, at least not to me."

"What do you mean?" demanded Emma.

"I didn't dare tell anyone, especially not my mother. But by the next day it drove me crazy until I had to tell someone, so I told Sally.

"Sally wasn't surprised because one night she went to bed early when I was still watching TV and woke up when she felt a hand slide inside her gown and down to her breast. It was Dad.

Scared out of her mind, she ran to the bathroom and locked the door and didn't come out until she heard me come to bed."

"Oh, Mary," said Emma, not knowing what else to say.

"Emma," Mary lamented, "my own father, my own dad."

"I've heard whispers from other girls about this kind of thing … but not *my* dad. And then to find out he molested Sally?" Anguish mixed with anger masked Mary's face. "At first I was confused, I couldn't believe it was happening. I thought maybe I just dreamed it. When it finally sunk in I was scared to death, and then I was sick … and I didn't know what to do."

"Did Sally tell anyone besides you?" asked Emma.

"No. But it gets worse. Sally and I decided we better talk to Pauline and Cora." Big tears welled up in Mary's eyes and rolled down her cheeks. She reached out and took Emma's hands and squeezed. "He did it to them too, only worse … "

Mary's father had been molesting Pauline and Cora over the last three months. Both little girls had kept it to themselves, scared to say anything. Who would believe them.

He started with Cora, the youngest and most vulnerable. Each time it happened in her own bed. He would lay down beside her and fondle between her legs.

"Both girls have been petrified, each thinking they were protecting the other," said Mary. "You should have seen the looks on their faces. They said he had put his finger up inside them, and it hurt so bad."

Emma pictured the two terrified girls laying in bed with their father abusing them. She couldn't bear it.

"Emma, what's almost worse is that we've been taught when in danger we should pray and God will always send help. But when Pauline and Cora prayed for God to make dad go away, or for someone to come save them, it didn't work …" Mary and Emma stared at each other in silence.

Finally Mary said she decided she had no choice but to tell her mother. In disbelief, Ruth finally confessed that deep down she had already suspected. While doing the washing, she had noticed spots of blood in the panties of the girls and hoped they belonged to Pauline who was near coming of age. Outraged, Mary's mother tearfully apologized to her girls for not facing the truth.

Ruth was as sweet a lady as could be found in or out of the fundamentalist lifestyle. Named after the biblical heroine of the Old Testament, she had been born and raised in the polygamist subculture, dutifully accepting the fundamentalist teachings. She went along with the obscurity and economic struggles that go with a big polygamous family, believing it was all part of the great cause, keeping alive a sacred religious tenet that would exalt her and her children in the next life beyond their wildest dreams.

She honored the priesthood as the ruling force in the group and believed the priesthood position that they were in constant communication with God, who would not allow the priesthood to lead the people astray. This was the security of her heart.

Ruth made the difficult decision to go to Richard Partridge, the prophet and president of the priesthood. His word was absolute and irrevocable. Her husband would have no choice but to obey a priesthood directive. Ruth took Mary with her and a pair of the bloody panties.

Richard Partridge received Ruth and Mary in the privacy of his office. Inviting them to make themselves comfortable, he smiled thinking they had questions about the marriage he presumed would be taking place, the marriage Mary's father had strongly encouraged.

Then their words poured forth. Sordid stories from both mother and daughter about husband and father, Ralph. Brother Partridge was visibly angry. Ruth and Mary felt reassured. Yes, they could trust the priesthood. Ralph would be dealt with.

When Ruth married Ralph she was seventeen, his third wife, and it was an arranged marriage. Ralph had just been put on the ruling council. Frank, another man on the council, approached Ralph and suggested they give each other one of their daughters for wife. Ralph got Ruth and Frank got a sixteen-year-old dishwater blonde from Ralph's first wife. Trading daughters for wives was not uncommon among polygamists in those days.

Richard Partridge could not hide his outrage. He glared first at Ruth and then at Mary.

He shouted, "You have accused one of my councilors, a man I completely trust, a man of God, of a heinous offense. What are you trying to do—ruin a good man's life? What is your true motive here? Is it jealously? "

Mary said, "I was stunned. Mother was speechless ... at first."

Emma was appalled, then angry. "How could a man who is supposed to be a prophet say such a thing?"

"Well, he did and, furthermore, he told us to keep quiet about it and not tell another living soul."

"What did your mother do?"

"I am so proud of her," said Mary forcing a defiant grin. "Mother has always been meek, too willing to compromise. I've never heard her raise her voice. But that day she shouted at Brother Partridge." The grin grew to a broad mischievous smile. "She yelled, 'I don't want that man in my house or near my girls ever again. And furthermore, I want a release, RIGHT NOW!' "

"You're kidding! What did Brother Partridge do?" asked Emma.

"He was so shocked he could hardly speak. He finally said he would talk to Daddy and he would pray and *think* about the release."

Sleepless night after night, Mary wandered the rooms of their house, checking on each of her sisters, making sure the doors were locked, watching a video until almost dawn hoping to finally sleep. Dark circles ringed her eyes and Emma and Gwen worried about their friend.

They spent hours reassuring her that she and her family were safe now that Richard Partridge had told Ralph not to visit Ruth's home until "this can be straightened out."

No longer able to pray, believing it must be a meaningless gesture, Mary agonized over the Heavenly Father in whom she had placed her complete trust. She watched her little sisters jump out of their skins over any loud noise and worried when they stayed close to their mother all day and evening rather than play with friends.

Her mother's sister-wives, having heard the whispers, brought delicious dishes of food, wanting to show love and concern. But it was awkward. They didn't know what to say except, "We love and appreciate you." To say more would have been a sin against their own husband.

Mary no longer took the sacrament on Sunday. How could

she, feeling the way she did about her dad—and Richard Partridge, the mouthpiece of God on earth.

June and July came and went. Ruth still hadn't received her release, which was the same as a divorcement, but only Richard Partridge had the power to grant it. Until then Ruth was eternally tied to Ralph. Without the release, she would be stuck with him forever. She prayed fervently for help from above.

Partridge took no action, afraid of what others would think—a wife being released from an apostle. He decided that Ruth's outburst was a one-time occurrence, and he could counsel her into compliance. But Ruth, more intrepid than ever, finally threatened to inform the whole group why she wanted the release, if it was not soon granted.

In spite of Partridge's desire to cover up the events, Ruth still believed deep in her soul that he held the keys to her salvation. Her indoctrination since childhood was thorough and complete. It permeated her very cells.

It never occurred to Ruth that Richard Partridge might be a fraud or a victim of his own delusions. And even if she had, what would she do, where would she go? The group was the only life she had ever known. Her friends and family were all in the group.

Determined though she was, courageous as she felt, Ruth had no choice but to wait on Richard Partridge. She had no way of knowing that other pedophile episodes in the group had come to Richard Partridge's attention.[4]

Ruth watched her children's despair, the girls frightened, the boys shamed. Mary worried her the most. A loving mother, devoted to her children, she prayed that Mary's feelings would somehow be healed. Mary was seventeen, soon she would marry. But how could she marry carrying this burden. How could she trust a man. And Ruth had nagging doubts that Mary had revealed all that had happened. She knew from other stories that children often reveal only a part of what actually happened to them.

Knowing her children needed medical attention and counseling gnawed at her, but she also knew the doctor would have to report it to the police, and there was no way she could do it secretly. The only therapist available to her as a polygamist was the "priesthood" and that meant she had to go through Richard

Partridge. So there was no help but God.

One day Ruth sat Mary down and gave her a stern talk. She explained that no one could change what had happened, that sometimes heartache comes to people unexpectedly, and each person finally had to choose how to deal with it. They could either become bitter and cynical, or they could place their trust in God and ask for help in bearing it.

Ruth affirmed her belief in the priesthood, even in Brother Partridge. She explained that any mortal person can make a mistake and it was Mary's job to forgive, and to embrace anew the doctrines of their belief with her whole heart. When one's resurrection and place in heaven depended on it, one could do most anything.

Chapter Seven

Each August the girls class headed for the mountains on an annual week long camp out. It was a gala, well talked about affair. Girls in the Partridge group as far north as Montana and as far south as Cedar City emigrated to Salt Lake just for the camp out. As many as fifty girls ages twelve to seventeen couldn't wait to head for the hills. It was a jubilee occasion and considered an opportunity to involve and indoctrinate girls like Emma, who were not particularly smitten with the group.

Preparations began three months in advance. The sisters, as they were called, took charge, overseen naturally by the priesthood. The sisters coaxed, begged, threatened, and groveled before the girls exhorting them to sign up no later than two weeks before the departure date, so they would know how much food to purchase. It was like pulling teeth even though it was the most talked about event of the year. Emma was one of the girls who couldn't make up her mind.

Gwen said, "Emma, you've got to come. It won't be any fun without you."

"What do they do up there," Emma asked, "sit around and tell Bible stories?"

"No," said Gwen. "We play games, go on hikes, eat a lot and talk. It's only the last night that's boring, when the priesthood comes up and gives us their *spiritual* talk."

"We divide up in groups of ten," said Mary, who had decided to go. "I have a big tent, it will hold our whole group. Each group has a den mother, and we're lucky, my cousin is our den mother."

Emma had landed a summer job as an office girl, thanks to a friend in their old neighborhood. She was learning skills that would help her land an even better job after she graduated from high school. Mary, Gwen, and Emma talked about finding good jobs, renting an apartment, and leaving the group behind—forever.

It was Mary who finally persuaded Emma to ask her boss if she could have a week off. Mary needed Emma to go, she needed her spunk and courage. To Emma's surprise, he was not upset, he even told her to have a good time and the job would be waiting when she got back.

The cost for each girl was $25.00 and some of the more affluent families donated money so the poorer girls could go.

Finally the big day arrived. The parking lot around the meeting hall was a jumble of vans, pick-up trucks and trailers. Fathers and husbands volunteered their help in transporting the tents, bedding, and food. One or two like Bruce were recruited and one or two others, young married men in their twenties, volunteered their time. Gwen suspected it was to look over potential wives.

The campground was located on the edge of a creek in the mouth of a small side canyon high above the town of Meadow. White pine and balsam flowed down the steep north slope merging comfortably with the shimmering quaking aspen. The ice cold water in the little rocky creek was clean and sweet. Small Brook Trout occasionally darted to the surface and grabbed a gnat.

The pleasant smell of burning pine drifted through the trees. The squawking of blue jays sounding like magpies with laryngitis and gray squirrels scolding usurpers echoed through the forest. But the darling varmints of the camp were the chipmunks, curious and trusting, coming within inches of little girls' delicate hands offering bits of bread and popcorn amidst a chorus of oooohs and ahhhhs and playful squeals.

The highlight of the camp was when Claudia and her gang challenged Gwen and her gang to a tug-of-war across the creek. Claudia naturally assumed that because her side was of noble birth and the most righteous, they were sure to win. Besides, there were twelve of them to only ten on Gwen's team.

The creek was five feet wide at the selected spot and ten inches deep. The rope was plenty long. Giving themselves an additional eight feet from the creek with which to maneuver, the girls took their places along the rope. Gwen and Claudia were the captains and first in line. Gwen sized up the opposition. Claudia's team not only outnumbered them but outweighed them. Two of the girls in the middle of the line weighed in excess of 200 pounds, their chubby faces and squinty eyes leering ominously, eager for the contest. Gwen and Claudia shouted encouragements over their shoulders.

"Let's show 'em who's the best," yelled Claudia.

"Let's give the blue bloods a bath," retaliated Gwen.

A den mother shouted, "Pull!" and the rope snapped taut. The girls on both sides yanked, pulled, tugged, grunted, screamed, broke wind, and shouted support to each other. Beads of sweat rolled down reddened cheeks. The girls pulled with all their might because it was more than a tug-of-war, it was a battle between good and evil, the superior against the inferior, the aristocrats against the plebeians, the lords against the vassals.

Claudia's crew was slightly stronger and Gwen found herself being slowly inched towards the creek. "Pull harder," she cried out over her shoulder. For a few seconds it was a standoff. Neither side moved and then responding to the pleas of Claudia, the obese girls grit their teeth, their faces turned crimson, and the gap between the creek and Gwen shortened.

Gwen set both feet like stakes at a 45 degree angle but it didn't help, her feet slid within two feet of the water's edge. And then both shoes struck and anchored to a large root half hidden in the grass. It was all it took. They were at loggerheads again, neither side budging.

Gwen concentrated on the two overweight girls. The leers had vanished, replaced by anxiety and stress, their blue eyes bulging. "Don't let up," urged Gwen. "They're getting tired. When I give the word, give it all you got."

"NOW!"

The sudden pull took the first fat girl by surprise. She lost her footing, let go of the rope and fell on her fanny. The second fat girl tripped over her chunky comrade and also fell, letting go of the rope. The five girls behind her tumbled on top of the fleshy heap. Before Claudia realized what had happened, she found herself flying through the air, landing on her belly in the creek. The other four girls catapulted after her, screaming at the top of their lungs.

Gwen, Emma, Mary, and the others were ecstatic, jumping around, hugging each other, screaming with delight. Gwen looked at the girls in the creek, all but Claudia were kicking, splashing, yelling for the others to jump in.

Claudia climbed to her feet, clothes stuck tight about her slim body, and with a scowl shook the water from her hands. She took a step and slipped on the rocks, falling on her backside. She sat there staring daggers at Gwen, who promptly came to attention and gave Claudia a Nazi salute. Then, impulsively, Gwen yelled, "Geronimo," and charged the creek, jumping in alongside the other girls. Emma and Mary followed. Within seconds, animosities between the two teams had been forgotten and all the girls were in the creek, laughing, screaming, splashing, hugging each other—except for Claudia and her two heavyweight friends, who stood contemptuously on the bank, hands on hips, water puddling beneath Claudia's feet.

Chapter Eight

The girls changed into a new outfit and hung their wet clothes on bushes and branches to dry. Gwen and her crew were left in camp, it was their turn to cook, while the others went hiking. The supper menu called for Sloppy Joe's, potato salad and pork'n beans.

Gwen's group counselor made assignments. Emma and two other girls were picked to peel potatoes. It was the easiest of all the jobs. The girls sat in folding chairs in the shade of quaking aspen next to the potato sack. The group counselor lugged over a large stainless steel pot half filled with water. A moment later one of the two camp directors moved a chair next to Emma and handed the girls paring knives, keeping one for herself.

The director was a pretty girl, self assured, five years older than Emma and three months pregnant. She was loads of fun and more like one of the girls than a director.

Her name was Lillian—tall, slender with dark waist-length hair combed to a high sheen. She seemed out of place with the other directors and counselors because of her expensive clothes, makeup, and sophisticated demeanor. Yet, she seemed to be true to the sacred principle of plural marriage.

That morning her husband, who happened to be Seth, the same princely Seth that had asked Emma to dance, flew over in his small single engine airplane and dropped Lillian a note attached to a small parachute made from a handkerchief. The ostentatious display caused quite a stir in the camp. Emma, Gwen, and a few others thought it romantic and applauded as the little parachute floated to the ground. But Claudia and her group of friends conspicuously ignored the romantic display, refusing to acknowledge that something romantic and affectionate had occurred.

Claudia's pious revulsion amused Gwen and Emma for they knew that Claudia and the others were secretly envious. Seth had made two passes, first buzzing the camp. All eyes lifted skyward and watched as the airplane made a slow sweeping circle carefully avoiding the mountain face.

Lillian couldn't contain her elation, waved and shouted, "IT'S SETH!" Then she turned to Emma and Gwen, "He said he was going to buzz the camp, but I didn't think he'd really do it." And then the airplane swooped over the camp and the little parachute popped open in its wake. As soon as Claudia and her group spotted the parachute they walked away.

Lillian ignored the reaction of the pious girls and shared the contents of the note with Gwen, Emma, and a dozen other girls who excitedly gathered around.

"Lillian, I love you. Seth."

Emma marveled at Lillian's poise, optimism, and ability to detach herself from the peer rejection of the elite group.

Handing Lillian a potato, Emma said, "Some of the girls weren't impressed, but I was."

Lillian chuckled, "I know."

"That doesn't bother you … the way the others reacted?" Emma asked.

"Not in the least," said Lillian with a smile.

"I've noticed you don't go out of your way to seek approval from the others," Emma said. "I like that. If I didn't know better, I would never think you were a polygamist."

Lillian chuckled again and tossed the peeled potato in the bucket. Emma handed her another. "Have you heard of Babylon?" Lillian asked.

Emma nodded.

"I'm going to tell you a little secret," said Lillian. "Most of the people in the group think everyone should practice stoicism. But down deep they're envious."

"What do you mean, stoicism?" asked Emma.

"In the group stoicism means the opposite of wicked, worldly Babylon," said Lillian. "In other words, they believe they should be passive and frugal in everything they do. Extravagance to them is wickedness so they avoid looking pretty or having nice things. Their goal is to be *plain*. They believe a proper polygamist should blend in unnoticed. Interestingly, what they think of themselves is anything but mundane and mediocre."

"So I've noticed," agreed Emma.

"But you know what," said Lillian, "there's nothing wrong with a little flamboyance once in awhile."

"Why are they like that?" asked Emma.

"They associate poverty, scarceness, and homeliness with humility." Lillian winked at Emma. "Take Brother Partridge for example. He has millions of dollars in tithing at his fingertips, but to look at him you'd think he was one step out of the poorhouse. That's what they want the gentiles to think."

"Are you sure?" asked Emma.

"Oh yes, I'm sure," said Lillian. "Seth is on the finance committee and has first hand knowledge of how the tithing is spent."

"But you're not like the others," said Emma. "You always look nice. You care how you look. And you don't worry about what others think."

"I'll accept that as a compliment," said Lillian with a smile. "But in some circles I would be thought of as flirting with sin, if not downright wicked."

"If you're so bad, why did they put you in charge of girls camp?"

"Because I get things done," answered Lillian with a smile. "In spiritual matters I'm overlooked, which is fine with me. The only meeting I attend is sacrament meeting, and only then when I feel like it, or it's the Sunday Seth is with me. Other than that, I'm pretty much my own girl."

Emma smiled approval.

Before they knew it, the potatoes had all been peeled. They lifted the pot of diced potatoes onto a butane black iron camp stove. Other girls had diced onions, celery, red radishes, and boiled eggs ready to mix with the potatoes, along with three large jars of mayonnaise. The Sloppy Joe's were simmering on another stove. The paper plates, pork'n beans, buns, chips, milk, and soda pop were ready. There was nothing else to do until the potatoes boiled.

"Let's take a little walk," Lillian suggested. "At this altitude it'll be a while before the potatoes are done."

Emma was flattered but a little suspicious. Lillian was an

enigma, a lovely nonconformist when compared with the people in the community. But Emma liked her very much and vowed to be her friend.

Taking a path that paralleled the creek, the girls breathed deeply and exhaled with exaggerated gratification. A gentle breeze shook the shimmering aspen leaves as their path narrowed through a patch of willows. On the other side was a deep pool at the base of a large boulder. From there the creek plunged down through mossy stones and fallen logs. The girls sat on a large square rock and watched as the water rippled into the pool, swirled, then slowed to glassy stillness.

Emma picked up a pebble and was about to toss it into the pool when a twelve-inch trout darted to the surface and grabbed a fly. The sight delighted them and they felt privileged to witness the remoteness, the beauty and even the ruthlessness of mother nature in action where one species feeds on another for survival. The glassy pool, the imposing mountains, the pines and the fresh clean cool air, all cleansed the mind and invigorated the body. It also nourished the intimacy of the moment and bonded friendships.

"How do you feel about polygamy?" asked Lillian.

"All my feelings are negative," said Emma. "I haven't seen anything to like about it. It's destroying my mother."

"I understand," said Lillian sincerely. "It's definitely not a lifestyle for everybody. But it needn't be a depressing, severe ordeal like you have observed. In many ways it can be rewarding."

"You mean rewarding in the next life," said Emma sarcastically. "I don't believe it. If it's a trial here it will be the same over there. Besides, I can't see a loving God requiring his people to be so miserable."

"What about Joseph Smith?" Lillian challenged. "What about the revelation and all that Brigham Young revealed? How do you deal with that?"

"I don't!" said Emma defensively. "I'm not building my life around Joseph Smith and Brigham Young or Richard Partridge. I'm going to build my life the way I want. I know right from wrong and polygamy is wrong for me."

"Well said," smiled Lillian. "At least you can think for yourself."

"I don't understand you, Lillian," remarked Emma cocking her head to one side. "You're not like the rest. Yet you're sharing a husband with three other women. You're pretty. You're smart and talented. You could have a man all to yourself."

Lillian smiled affectionately. She reached over and patted Emma's arm. The trout jumped again making a splash, distracting from the reverie. They laughed. And then Lillian became very serious. "Are we friends?" she asked.

"I'd like to be your friend," said Emma, "but not a plural wife."

"Then I'm going to tell you something I've never told anyone else. That is, if it can be just between the two of us?"

"You have my word," said Emma, sensing that something very special was about to be revealed.

"I chose to be a plural wife because I like the arrangement," said Lillian and waited for the remark to sink in.

"What about Joseph Smith," said Emma, astonished.

"Phooey on Joseph Smith," said Lillian with a mischievous grin, her teeth flashing in the dimming light. The trout jumped again. The pleasant smell of burning pine from a log fire filtered through the trees. "If I were to believe everything Joseph Smith allegedly said," Lillian continued cautiously, "I would be a robot just like most of the other women, groveling at the feet of the priesthood, competing with sister-wives for time with Seth, or resigning myself to a secondary life of perfunctory affection."

"Now you've got me all mixed up," said Emma. "Explain."

"Look at it this way," she began, "I have more freedom than a monogamous wife. I would hate to have a man around every minute of the day telling me what to do, snooping into my personal affairs. So, in a sense, I have the best of two worlds. I have a business of my own, a dress shop, that I manage the way I want. Seth doesn't interfere. I purchased it with an inheritance and Seth has nothing to do with it. I know of other women who have inherited large sums of money and right away the husband takes charge and manages the money, because it's his priesthood prerogative. Well, that won't happen with me."

Emma was transfixed and listened intently.

"Men are polygamous by nature. It's rare for a man with an adventurous spirit to bridle his roving eyes or keep his pants zipped. At least I know who Seth is with and I even get to help pick them. Seth can't take a plural wife without my approval, or the approval of the other wives."

Lillian continued to talk while Emma listened with intense amazement. "When Seth comes to my house it's all quality time. Each visit is like a reunion or a date. We might go to a show, a restaurant, or I might prepare a candlelight dinner. Whatever we do, we keep the honeymoon alive—like Seth dropping a love note from an airplane. And I decide when to have children and how many. It's my body, but that doesn't mean I don't enjoy the intimacy and bonding of a marriage, if you know what I mean."

"But isn't that kind of like being a mistress?" Emma said as delicately as she could.

"I guess you could look at it that way, but I see myself as one of four families. I have one child by a previous marriage, one by Seth and another on the way. I'll stop at three. When I need Seth, he's there. He treats both children the same. Whatever other people might think, I have a family, the love of a good man, and my independence. And there is one other plus—the adventure. My life is an adventure. Growing flowers, cutting lawns, Sunday School, lost in the obscurity of a subdivision, that's fine for other women, but not me. I want more out of life. I look at the women who come into my shop and spend hundreds of dollars thinking my dresses are going to enrich and brighten their lives. Some have boyfriends on the side. Some are bored stiff. Some are so worried about their security they're afraid to rock the marriage boat; the only excitement they get out of life is reading Steven King, a romance novel, or watching James Bond on television."

"But what about religion? What about Brigham Young and Joseph Smith?" asked Emma.

"Religion is about halfway down the list in my priorities," Lillian confided. "And if the other women who have converted to Mormon fundamentalism were honest with themselves, religion would be halfway down their list also. You see, it's not religion per se, I mean the doctrines of exaltation and resurrection in an afterlife, that induce people to convert, it's what religion offers in this life. I've thought it over very carefully; most women convert for the security. In this group, a woman can choose the family where she thinks she belongs. If the family is financially able, they must accept her. It doesn't cost her a dime and she has all the security of a wife of twenty years."

Lillian stood and stretched. "It's different with men who convert," she said. "They must have something worthwhile to give to the priesthood, like tithing. The women get in free, the men have to pay. Also, men are motivated by power and sex. When you think about it, power and sex are synonymous. Religion is just the excuse for deviating from the norm."

She sat back down and studied Emma for a second, looking for some reaction. Seeing nothing negative, she continued. "I live plural marriage because it meets my needs. All the rest is hyperbole. At least I'm honest with myself. But you wouldn't be able to whip the truth out of a born and groomed polygamist. They're so brain washed they think sour milk is ice cream. Don't even try to discuss what I have said with them. Just go along with the tide. That's why I seldom attend any meetings. When I do, it's all I can do to listen to all that priesthood junk."

"I don't know what to say," said Emma.

"Don't say anything, not to anyone, especially about what I just said. The people in the group are happy with their delusion of superiority. Allow them to believe they are God's chosen people, it's a boost to their self-esteem and most of them can use it. As a rule they are harmless and hardworking. It's the parasites and predators in the priesthood that I can't stand. They suck up tithing like vampires and squander it away on stupid get-rich-quick schemes. Sometimes I worry about Seth."

"What do you mean?" asked Emma

"Seth likes to live on the edge. Maybe that's why I'm attracted to him. I don't ask questions, but I suspect his oil exploration business is on the shady side. So far he hasn't hit any oil that I know of, but he's sold an awful lot of stock. He runs what is known as a boiler room, that's a lot of people crammed in a little room talking on telephones selling stock. They work on the numbers system, like out of fifty calls they can expect one big sale."

Emma recalled that she hadn't seen Lillian at the dance the time she first met Seth. She wondered why? The other three wives appeared to be in perfect harmony with each other. Could it be possible that Lillian didn't get along with the other wives?

"I don't mean to be personal," said Emma. And then she thought, what I'm about to ask is personal. "I guess I do mean to be a little personal," corrected Emma, "I hope you don't mind. But, how do you get along with your sister-wives? I mean, you seem so independent."

Lillian smiled. "I don't mind at all. It's a subject every polygamist woman should discuss. Because if you can't get along with your sister-wives, you're in for a hell-of-a lot of trouble. You'll never last." Lillian's smile broadened. "I get along very well with my sister-wives. In fact, they work with me at my dress shop. Notice I said they work *with* me, not for me. That's the key. If one sister-wife places herself above another, there's going to be trouble. You may not be together all the time, but when you are, it's imperative you treat each other with respect and equality. My sister-wives are fun, like you; we get together just the four of us and go to lunch and enjoy each other. Sometimes we conspire against Seth and play tricks on him."

Laughter and screams resounded through the trees. "I think the girls are back from their hike," said Lillian.

They got to their feet and impulsively looked at the pool of water. "Good-bye, Mr. Fish," said Emma. As if on cue, the trout made a mighty leap in the air exposing a crimson streak that ran the length of his body. He twisted gracefully and dove back in the water head first.

"The grand finale," said Lillian with delight.

They slowly picked their way back up the path savoring the precious moments of female comradery and confession. Emma was more than pleased with her special new friend even though she was not sure she agreed with Lillian in every detail. At least she was honest and realistic. Emma felt she had matured a couple years during their talk.

"Are there any more men like Seth and women who think as you do?" asked Emma.

"I'm sure there are," she replied. "You can tell by the way they behave and dress. Our group, as you probably already know, is the most liberal of all the fundamentalist groups. The women are not as oppressed and used up as in the other groups. Consequently, some women are quite independent and creative … "

Emma interrupted, "Like you."

"Yes, like me but in different ways. Some own their own businesses and are very productive, but others achieve positions of power. Remind me to tell you about Mary Pugmire. You know who she is, don't you?"

"Yeah," said Emma, "she's the one they call the grand matriarch."

Lillian chuckled. "That's the one. But she's actually a very intelligent and good woman. I like her."

They strolled out of the forest and onto the edge of the small meadow and camp. Claudia was the first to spy them and pointed, yelling, "There they are!" as if they had just been caught doing something naughty. "Come on," Claudia yelled again, "we're waiting to say a blessing on the food."

As they approached the hungry group milling around the camp stoves intimidating the cooks, Emma whispered, "Are there more adventurers like Seth?"

"You mean loveable scoundrels?" Lillian whispered back with a smile. "Yes, a cadre, and they're all part of Richard Partridge's inner circle."

Chapter Nine

Emma and Lillian were last in the dinner line. They approached Gwen who was dishing out the potato salad. "Where you guys been?" Gwen asked.

"Watching the fish jump," replied Emma.

The campground was a litter of girls sitting on rocks and logs with plates heaped with food. The sun dropped behind the mountain and the air turned chilly. One girl left her seat long enough to toss a log on the campfire. Emma by her side, Lillian surveyed the campground looking for a place to sit.

"By the way," said Lillian casually, "Seth would like to date you. He thinks you would make a lovely addition to the family."

Emma was not surprised or disappointed. *I should be outraged but I'm not.* If anything she was flattered and wondered what had come over her. Maybe it was being compared with Lillian and placed on the same level. She found the surrogate proposal amusing and was pleased with how well she kept her composure. But she couldn't help wondering if Lillian's sudden friendship and frank girl to girl talk had something to do with Seth's interest in her. She remembered Gwen's words at the dance, "If one of Seth's wives suddenly takes an interest in you, that means Seth wants you for a wife."

Several girls moved closer to the bonfire, vacating a log on the far side of the camp. Emma said, "There's a place we can sit."

As they started towards the log, Lillian, still relaxed, and apparently unconcerned, said, "What shall I tell him?"

Impulsively, Emma said, "Tell him I have gonorrhea."

Lillian froze in her tracks and burst out laughing, nearly dropping her plate of food. The other girls in camp turned to see what was so funny.

"Tell him anything that will put me out of his mind," Emma

continued. "Tell him I'm a witch. Tell him I'm a demon from outer space."

Lillian couldn't stop laughing. She started for the log, balancing the plate in her hand. When they reached the log, Lillian had regained her composure. "Good girl," she said. "I think I like you much better as a friend than a sister-wife. Although I have to admit, Seth has good taste in women."

Emma was relieved. She was afraid she might have offended Lillian. And now she valued their friendship even more.

Gwen, Mary, and three other girls approached with full plates of food. "What's so funny?" asked Gwen.

Emma didn't expect Lillian to share the story but she did. Gwen also found it hilarious and patted Emma on the back saying, "I can't wait to use that one myself." Mary and the other girls, more reserved, just snickered.

"I don't know what made me say that," confessed Emma. "It just came out. I'm really quite embarrassed."

The other camp director called the girls to order. "Tonight is testimony night girls. I want you all to get serious and think about the many blessings God has given you. Then I want you to stand and share your thoughts with the rest of us. Tonight is a special night. We are so fortunate to have these beautiful mountains, a place we can go and enjoy ourselves, and reflect upon our approbations."

The mood of the group immediately turned sedate and they moved closer to the fire. A few pulled coats up around necks. Testimony meetings were common among the fundamentalists. There was never any reason to assign people to bear their testimony, there were always plenty of volunteers.

It was now dusk, the mountains with jagged images of pine trees on the horizon were silhouetted in the background. The first to rise was a heavyweight girl dressed in bib overalls. The side of her face shadowed, she looked skyward at the stars beginning to appear. Then her gaze fell to the ground and a tear trickled down her cheek.

Emma listened with genuine empathy as the girl thanked her Heavenly Father, thanked her parents, and thanked the priesthood. The girl sobbed and thanked the camp directors and the girls' counselors, and Brother Partridge, and sobbed some more.

Emma studied the girl, a sweet, kind, talented young lady plagued with genetic obesity. Both her mother and father were fat. Biologically she didn't stand a chance. Yet she was as charming and accommodating as a girl could be. She had the makings of an excellent mother and wife, but in a monogamous society where physical beauty opens doors of privilege, she would be hard pressed to find a mate worthy of her creative talents and decency. But in the group she would be well received where litheness was not a condition of acceptance. Besides, she came from a stalwart, well-bred family. Emma decided she would probably be more productive and happy as a polygamist, provided her husband was not one of those tyrants who would not allow her personality to blossom and flourish.

Lillian was only slightly affected by the spirit of the gathering. She had been to many testimonials before and each one was very much the same, lots of thank you's and crying. Some of the girls were deeply sincere and some, like their adult counterparts, used the testimony to make points with their superiors.

After the third litany of weeping thank you's, Lillian whispered to Emma, "I dare you to bear your testimony."

"Who would want to hear from a girl with gonorrhea?" Emma replied smugly. "Why don't you tell me about Mary Pugmire, the grand matron of the group?"

"Oh dear," answered Lillian in fun, "you've not only turned into a licentious nymph but a hopeless gossip."

"I learned it all from my camp director." They both muffled their snickers so as not to disturb the others; but Gwen, who was extremely bored, discerned their mischief and moved closer.

"What I'm about to tell you," Lillian began, "is not meant to be critical but to let you know that a clever, charming woman can work her way into a position of power and security even in a polygamist group where women are supposed to be oppressed."

"Right on," said Gwen. "Women are smarter than men. Look what Delilah did to Samson."

Lillian continued, "There are strong women and weak women, both in polygamy and in the outside world, just as there are dumb women and brainy ladies ... like Mary Pugmire. A few men dislike her because of her power and refer to her as the high priestess. And among the ambitious but weak women, she is envied—and they say she's just lucky. But luck has nothing to do with it. Mary is a skilled, resourceful lady and deserves to be on top. As a result she is loved, admired ... and hated. But everybody respects her, even her enemies."

"So how did she do it," asked Gwen.

"Mary was converted to the principle from the Mormon Church. Her monogamous husband was an abuser. She was introduced to the group by a lady friend and from there, started to study. Her conversion to fundamentalism was not a sudden leap. She took her time, analyzing, learning all she could about the customs and rules, especially the unwritten rules that are often the most important."

"Like what?" asked Emma.

"The pecking order," said Lillian. "The people with the most influence. Who to suck up to and how. Who among the apostles is secure and who isn't. Who is ambitious, who is a back stabber. She learned about the people, their likes and dislikes, until she could read them like a psychologist."

Lillian took a deep breath and glanced around to see if anyone was listening. "I'm going to tell you another secret," she said. "You don't get ahead in this world by just being sweet and nice, you get ahead by making something happen."

Their talking started to annoy a few of the girls who were dutifully concentrating on the testimonies, so Lillian and the girls backed away into the shadows.

"Anyway," continued Lillian, "Mary wisely chose the family she wanted to join. Love had nothing to do with it. She picked an ambitious apostle with money and property who is rumored to have bought his way onto the council. The apostle immediately recognized her keen intellect, knowledge of the scriptures, and showed her off to Richard Partridge. Before long she was Brother Richard's personal secretary."

"Smooth move," said Gwen.

"That's not all," said Lillian. "She gathered around her an entourage of like-minded wives and they used their influence to help mold the group into what it is today. Of all the fundamentalist groups, the women in this group have much more freedom and input into the decisions of the priesthood than any other. And you can thank Mary Pugmire. You can also thank her for the Relief Society, the Girls Class, and girls camp. If the truth were known, she has influenced more priesthood decisions than the rest of the apostles combined. In my opinion," Lillian said with a chuckle, "most of Richard Partridge's success as a prophet can be traced to Mary. In fact, this group would do better if *she* were the president of the priesthood."

Gwen impulsively let out a whoop, and then quickly put a hand over her mouth. When no one around the campfire seemed to notice, she said, "I can see it now, Mary dressed in black tights with five husbands and a bull whip."

"But how did she do it?" asked Emma.

"With charm, gentle persuasion, greater intellect, and the power of suggestion," said Lillian. "A woman has more resources at her disposal than a man, if she knows how to use them."

"Gather around, girls," called the spiritual camp director. "Susan is going to sing for us." Lillian was sure the call was meant for her. She, Emma, and Gwen were the only girls not already gathered.

They moved closer. Susan was standing by the fire, her head bowed in humility. She was petite, shy with a coquettish smile, and well proportioned. Susan had taken professional singing lessons and had sung in a semi-classical opera at the University of Utah. She had just turned eighteen, looked sixteen, and from all indications had a great musical future.

Emma had never heard Susan sing and in scrutinizing her demeanor, standing humbly in the firelight, looking very ordinary, she wondered if Susan was really as good as her reputation. Mormons had a tendency in their attempt to be positive, to use the word "great" when describing only mediocre deeds and talents. But in Susan's case, her laurels were not exaggerated. Her voice was as clear and crisp as a Jerusalem bell, the words perfectly articulated. Before she had completed the first stanza, little Susan had captured the heart and soul of the group.

Her first song was a hymn, "Oh My Father." It was a perfect

setting. The shadows, the gurgle of the creek, leaping flames from the bonfire, all blended harmoniously with Susan's strong, rich soprano voice.

When Susan finished her second song, a unique rendition of "The Lord's Prayer," there wasn't a dry eye in camp. She ended her medley on a positive note by singing "Summertime," from George Gershwin's opera, *Porgy and Bess*. When she finished, the campground was deadly silent except for the gentle lapping of water from the creek. And then the calm exploded with applause.

Susan thanked the girls and before she mingled with her admirers she made an announcement.

"I would like everyone to know that two weeks from tomorrow night...." her head ducked in embarrassment, "... I will be sealed to Emmett Johnson." She lifted her pretty head. Her eyes sparkled in the firelight. "You're all invited," she squealed and disappeared in the crowd amidst sighs, well wishes, and congratulations.

Emma looked at Gwen and said, "She has the most beautiful voice I have ever heard. She's so tiny, you would never ever guess it was her singing. And she is darling. I could listen to her all day."

"I know," agreed Gwen, "she's so talented … I don't know why she's wasting her time around here." Gwen hesitated and then said, "Yes, I do know why. She's been programmed into thinking she has to be a plural wife."

"Who's Emmett Johnson?" asked Emma. "And how many wives does he have?"

"Susan will be the second wife," Gwen said gloomily. "His first wife is a blue blood. I don't know much about him. I heard he's a real brain, good looking, and in law school."

Chapter Ten

It was Friday. That morning the girls ran potato bag races, learned to tie knots with a new manila rope so stiff it would hardly bend, and then they were taken on a short hike and taught how to tell the difference between deer and sheep tracks. After lunch the time was spent tidying up camp in preparation for the Brother Richard Partridge and his apostles.

The appearance and presence of the priesthood was supposed to be the highlight and most spiritual evening of the camp. It was this final event that the spiritual camp director worried about most, how to make the welcoming of the priesthood a momentous milepost, worthy of their omniscient message. If she had access to a band, she would be like the pioneer saints of the city Tooele in the 1850s.

When Brigham Young came to visit and preach, the Tooele City officers, who were usually the bishop and his counselors, would ride out ten miles from town to an outcropping called 'lookout rock' and intercept the prophet's caravan of wagons, shaded coaches, bodyguards, and company of finely groomed horseman. An impressive troop of mounted town folk would follow. From there Brigham and his loyal courtiers would be escorted into town led by the band playing "We Thank Thee Lord For Our Prophet." Sadly, she had no band.

But she did place all the folding chairs reserved for the priesthood on both sides of the fire with the plan that their faces would be illuminated. A ready supply of wood was neatly stacked preparatory to feeding the fire, maintaining just the right blaze. The best meal, hamburgers, and boiled chicken smothered in cream of mushroom soup, was reserved for Friday night. Lillian was in charge of cooking and serving. The priesthood would be served on agate-blue tin plates with real silverware.

Richard Partridge customarily brought with him from four to

eight apostles. On rare occasions he brought one of his wives, usually Beth, his favorite. It was never known how many to expect. Like everything else, plans were impromptu, by the spirit. An apostle might find out an hour ahead of time that Brother Richard desired his presence.

The spiritual camp director reserved a chair for herself next to the apostles and invited Lillian to sit next to her, knowing that she would decline.

Like clockwork the two automobiles arrived an hour and a half before sunset. The party totaled nine. To their surprise, Mary Pugmire exited from the back of the second car with blue denim dress, her hair pulled back in a bun, and no makeup. The two youngest apostles were in the car with Mary. One was Don, a tall good looking man in his forties. The other was Rupert, a ferret-like man also in his forties, who had that icy look of uncompromising resolve and a smirk that said, "I know you're up to something, you can't fool me." And then there was Eldon, a man unyielding, opinionated, guiltless, and militant. He was credited with driving several undesirables out of the group.

Colleen's father rode with Partridge, no surprise. Another apostle Ken, in his early sixties with thick gray hair that needed cutting, was the driver. When he climbed out of the car, he stood there with a cheesy grin.

Behind him was Dan, nicknamed Dangerous Dan because he was continually attempting to seduce converts into investing in his get-rich-quick real estate ventures. He had everybody believing he was a champion entrepreneur, including Partridge, and had managed to squander hundreds of thousands of priesthood money on high risk ventures. No one could figure out how he retained the confidence of Brother Partridge.

The apostles had dressed for the occasion, plaid long-sleeved shirts except for Brother Maynard Courtland, who was never seen without a dress shirt, usually white. Today he was roughing it and wore no tie. But Brother Partridge, dapper on all occasions, sported a beige tie with a picture of a male Mallard duck in flight. As usual Mary was her stately self, but mollifying and deferent to the great men around her.

On that Friday night, the apostles all had one thing in common, a toothy smile that said they were glad to be there, except for Eldon. He smiled but no teeth showed. It was the best he could do.

After all the salutes and greetings were over, the apostles were guided to the food where they heaped their plates full.

Dangerous Dan took a deep breath and with theatric gusto said, "Boy, this mountain air gives a man an appetite." It caught the attention of the rest who nodded in agreement. He then made a show of devouring the food and complementing the girl's cooking while scooping up a second helping. After he gorged himself, he sought out his nieces and granddaughters and told each one, "I sure love you!" Emma was impressed, in spite of herself.

The bonfire was kindled. The sun dropped behind the mountain leaving in its wake a red sunset. Girls grabbed for sweaters and coats as the south wind continued to blow through the quaking aspen. The apostles toothy smiles were replaced by visages of supreme responsibility and wisdom as they strolled towards their chairs. It was the cue for all to gather around. Lillian, Emma, Gwen, Mary, and three other girls lagged behind so they could be on the outer row.

The apostles took their places. Brother Partridge stood in front of the chair next to the fire. His countenance contrite and solemn, he faced the congregation and surveyed the pretty faces. All eyes were on him. He asked Brother Eldon to say the opening prayer.

Brother Eldon called upon the angels in heaven, with drawn swords, to protect the camp while the president of God's priesthood and the apostles of the Lord Jesus Christ addressed the congregation. The spirit inspired him to inform the girls how fortunate they were to have the priesthood as their mentor and the scriptures to guide them into motherhood. He praised God, Joseph Smith, Brigham Young, John Taylor, Lorin Woolley, and Richard Partridge.

With his kind, grandfatherly demeanor, Brother Partridge again stood and with a jaunty smile told the girls how wonderful it was to be in the mountains next to God's wonderful creations, to be speaking to these wonderful girls, and how he dearly loved each and every one of them. He praised the camp directors, the camp counselors, and the girls themselves. He spoke with sincerity, emitting genuine love. The introduction was short and sweet.

The sunset had faded into blackness as a toenail moon peeked above the mountains in the east. One of the counselors lighted two butane lanterns.

"I have a pleasant surprise," Brother Partridge said, the jaunty smile spreading across his face. "I've brought sister Mary with us as a special treat. I would like her to say a few words."

Mary rose to her feet as Partridge sat down. "Well," she said, "this is as much a surprise to me as it is to you." She glanced quickly at Brother Partridge, flashing him a smile. "Brother Richard only gave me ten minutes notice. Nevertheless, I am honored to be here among you girls, because whether you realize it or not, you girls are the treasure of this group. You are the mothers of the future. Your sons will inherit the priesthood and one day they will sit where these great men now sit." She stretched both arms out, acknowledging the men on both sides of the fire.

"Do not underestimate," she continued, "the importance of your calling as mothers and helpmates in Zion. Your responsibility is as great as that of the priesthood. Your nurturing and guidance will prepare your sons for the challenges of the future. Your training and example will prepare your daughters to be mothers of future priesthood holders. Remember the words of Brigham Young who said, 'when you send a man to college you only educate one man. But when you send a woman to college, you educate a whole family.'

"The priesthood needs you. Your husbands need you. Without a husband you cannot go to the celestial kingdom, and without a wife, there is no need for a man to go to the celestial kingdom. The gospel of Jesus Christ has no meaning without women. The temples were built so men could marry women. The women are the backbone of the Church. "

Gwen was squirming with delight. "Way to go, Mary Pugmire," she whispered to anyone that could hear. "You're a feminist through and through."

Emma was also moved by Mary. Her poise and casual delivery made the words more impressive. And she was absolutely right, at least about the importance of women, especially among polygamist men. In essence she was telling these young girls how much latent power they held. Now she understood more what Lillian was trying to say, that even in a male dominated society, a smart, enterprising woman had political, cultural, and sensual assets at her disposal. Polygamy needn't be a totally female subservient society.

"And in conclusion," Mary Pugmire said, "the Church is to the Priesthood what the wife is to the husband. Remember girls, you are the Church—do your job—but respect and honor the priesthood."

Emma was impressed. *A great ending Mary. Let them think they're in charge.*

Mary humbly took her seat next to Partridge. It was Don's turn next.

"Mary Pugmire is a class act hard to follow. But Mary is right," he stammered, "you girls are special. Soon, many of you will be getting married and it's important that you marry a man with priesthood. Marry a man that will have the power to resurrect you the morning of the First Resurrection. Marry a man that can take you to the Celestial Kingdom."

The spirit was strong and Don shifted into high gear. "There are other groups that claim to have the priesthood, but they're usurpers, charlatans, deceivers—the priesthood is with this group and Richard Partridge is the president of the priesthood. How do we know? Because we are the only people on earth living all of God's laws. Because God has told Brother Partridge that we are his people, and the gentiles and usurpers, the other fundamentalists—those that refuse to recognize the true priesthood—will have to face Brother Partridge in the next life before they hope to meet Jesus Christ. It is what is known as the Law of Introduction. No mortal can escape it."

Gwen whispered to Emma, "Don't worry, I'll put on a fake mustache and introduce you."

Dangerous Dan was the next speaker, and it only took him nine minutes to put half the girls to sleep, and would have put the other half to sleep if the wind hadn't changed. The wind swooped down from the north and Rupert tossed three logs on the fire creating a smoke that blew in Brother Partridge's face. The prophet waved his hand back and forth but it did no good. The apostles on the windward side of the fire craned their necks to watch their leader as Mary fanned smoke out of their faces.

The girls enjoyed the smoky comedy, as they called it, and were wide awake when Brother Partridge delivered the final momentous speech. Brother Partridge was not an eloquent speaker but made up for his lack of sophistication with a conspicuous display of humility and simple sincerity. It was a style he had mastered to perfection. For fifteen minutes he praised his beautiful, faithful, queenly wives, convincing the empathetic girls that he loved his wives more than any other man could love a wife, and wept with joy to prove it. Afterwards, Rupert said the closing prayer. Ten minutes after that, Partridge and his entourage were racing down the canyon, anxious to get home before it got too late.

That night laying in her sleeping bag, Emma reflected on the entire evening. She found herself comparing Partridge and his apostles to the president of the Mormon Church and his twelve apostles. She had watched LDS General Conference with her parents on television many times and was familiar with the cultured, responsible image of those men, mostly university graduates and highly successful businessmen who were contributing their talents to the Church. The contrast was humiliating.

But she wanted to be fair. She knew that other than Dangerous Dan, who had a formal education, the polygamist apostles were self-educated men who necessarily might lack polish and poise. But more often than not, their speeches seemed to be attempts to persuade the listeners that, indeed, they really did have authority.

Or perhaps they're just trying to convince themselves.

Emma yearned for her old days in the Mormon Church. Yes, they taught that the father in the home, the priesthood holder, should lead their families and have the final say on major decisions. But the men were also counseled to listen carefully to their wives' opinions before making that final decision. And Emma knew that in the homes of many of her old friends, decisions were a joint effort between the parents; that's how it really was. Then she realized that this had been the case in her home as well, even though her mother always made the point that "your dad makes the final decisions." Maybe that was just her way of teaching her children to respect his priesthood. And, maybe never before had her parents had such a difficult thing to deal with. Maybe it took her mother so by surprise, she fell into the years-old teaching that the husband had the final say.

Very confusing.

This subject put aside, Emma's thoughts turned to the week of camp. Claudia and her friends had provided a sharp contrast to the dozen other girls, the ones not in Emma's own clique. Living with them, working and playing together in a raw environment, had been fun. Emma admitted to herself that maybe she had been hasty in condemning all the girls outside her own little group as simple-minded polygamist kids. These particular girls seemed more free and happy than she had given them credit for. Perhaps it was their family life that made the difference. Maybe it was the dad or the mom. Until now, her entire focus had been on her dad and Colleen, her mother's abandonment, Mary's wretched dad, the priesthood leaders, and all the other negatives that grabbed her attention.

Maybe there were positives she had refused to notice. Maybe polygamy actually worked well for some people. Clearly it did for Lillian and Mary Pugmire.[5] She could understand Gwen wanting out, and certainly Mary. But she could see there were other girls, seemingly happy girls, who appeared to look forward to plural marriage. And maybe those were the girls whose fathers were kind and thoughtful of their wives.

She finally concluded that there were as many girls with varying attitudes in this group as there were in the outside world.

But it's still not for me.

As summer gave way to autumn, Emma, Gwen, and Mary became seniors and stayed scholastically at the top of their class. In the windows of department stores, images of ghosts, witches, and black cats had been replaced by turkeys, pilgrims, and pumpkin pies. Susan, with the beautiful voice, had wed her lawyer husband and was now pregnant.

To her relief, Ruth finally got her release, offered up grateful prayers, and was looking for a new family to enter. At least on the surface, Mary seemed to be doing better. She was able to sleep, but she still checked on her sisters every night after making sure the doors were locked. And she had started praying again. But she still wanted to leave the group.

Chapter Eleven

Gene worked like a slave every second of his spare time in completing Colleen's part of the Four-Plex. After Colleen moved in and settled, she designated one of the bedrooms as a nursery and couldn't wait to decorate. She was five months pregnant and happy.

Gene wanted the family to eat Thanksgiving dinner at Colleen's. Emma didn't want anything to do with Colleen, sitting with her at sacrament meeting was bad enough. But Gene's reasoning was sound. There simply wasn't enough room in Connie's trailer for the whole family. Gene was trying hard to keep his family unified.

Since the wedding, Emma had been stifling her resentment for the sake of peace. Colleen sensed the resentment and tried to win Emma's love and support whenever she could. But when Emma put her mind to it, she could be a real snot.

In Emma's mind, Thanksgiving dinner was the most sacred holiday of the year, more sacred than Christmas. Ever since she could remember the family had eaten Thanksgiving dinner with her mother's parents. After all, they were still welcome there and to have dinner at Colleen's would be like forsaking her grandparents. She decided to voice her ill feelings to her mother.

"I don't care what Daddy thinks," said Emma. "This is going too far. Why can't we go to Grandpa and Grandma's and Dad and Colleen can go wherever they want?"

"Because it wouldn't be fair to your father," rebuked Connie. "He's worked so hard to finish the Four-Plex. Your grandparents will understand. And, Emma, since Gene's parents are so hostile to us now, he wants to establish his own home."

Her mother's reaction surprised Emma. It had been awhile since they had sat down and had a woman to woman talk. Had her mother changed? Was she starting to accept all this polygamy stuff?

Eight months had passed since Gene and Connie converted to Mormon fundamentalism. It was not an easy transition. Connie had no marketable skills such as shorthand, but she did have intelligence, an enchanting personality, and intense desire. Going to work as an office girl in a large real estate office, she emerged six months later as a licensed real estate saleswoman. Entering the real estate industry had affected Connie like a magic potion. Her old cheerfulness returned. Her eyes flashed with a gleam of self-reliance. She gave old clothes away and purchased a complete new wardrobe of dresses and suits consistent with the apparel of an upcoming, ambitious real estate dynamo. And when she went to work, she was stunning. Her demeanor epitomized success, but she was neither arrogant or overbearing. Of Connie's many attributes, knowing how to dress and behave were at the top of the list. At work she was a foxy amiable lady. But at home she was a condescending, conforming wife. Her apparent acquiescence to the polygamist lifestyle puzzled and worried Emma, and she was disappointed when her mother didn't side with her concerning Thanksgiving Day.

The steaming succulent turkey, stuffed with onion, celery and breaded dressing, was roasted in Colleen's brand new GE range. When she opened the oven door, the mouth-watering aroma filled the kitchen and floated through every room. From the hot drippings, Colleen made a tasty brown gravy, a recipe from her grandmother. Connie and Emma furnished the trimmings. Mashed potatoes, yams, Jell-O, celery sticks stuffed with cream cheese, whole kernel corn, green and black pearl olives, hot rolls, pickle relish, cranberry sauce, and pumpkin pies topped with whipped cream.

The table was set with a white linen tablecloth. The silverware, napkins, and water glasses were all new, never used wedding presents from Colleen's first marriage. She had gone the extra mile to make it a special day, and Connie was grateful.

Emma looked around the apartment. Everything conservative and functional, with no frilly lamp shades or statuettes, no lovely vases. There was not even a landscape painting to break up the monotony; just an etching of Jesus Christ and Joseph Smith, and on the mantel a photograph of Richard Partridge.

Gene sat at the head of the table, Connie on his right, Colleen on his left. Emma was at the opposite end of the table facing her dad. Keith and Colleen's baby were in between. Everyone was uptight. It was their first time together without dozens of people around. Gene racked his brain for something to say that would put everyone at ease. Out of desperation he said, "Boy, that turkey's good."

Emma, empathizing with his discomfort said, "Yes, it is. Good job, Colleen."

"Yeah, real good," said Keith who was gnawing on a drumstick.

"Thanks," said Colleen. "That new oven works like a dream."

Then, out of the clear blue, Colleen said, "Congratulations, Connie."

"Congratulations?" answered Connie. "Whatever for?"

"Your first big sale," Colleen answered smugly. "You know, the condominium."

Connie glanced at Gene. "I'm afraid congratulations are a little premature. We're still negotiating. It will be a while before we close, if we close."

"That's great news," said Emma excitedly. "How come you haven't said anything?"

Connie turned toward Emma. "I didn't want to get anybody's hopes up. You know, count the chickens before they've hatched."

"But do you think you'll make the sale?" asked Emma.

"It looks good, but as I said, it's not certain. The contract is complicated. The broker is helping me with the difficult parts and when that's through, the buyer's attorney will want to review it. Anything could happen. So it might be several months before I know anything for certain."

"What kind of commission does a real estate agent get?" asked Colleen.

Connie realized that if Colleen knew she had a sale in the making, she also knew what the commission was. She shot a quick glance at Gene, the only person she had told. Embarrassed, he pretended to be eating. He had assumed that Colleen would treat their conversations as confidentially as Connie always had.

"It's usually six percent," Connie said casually.

"Six percent," said Colleen enthusiastically. "Wow, that condo must be worth several million. That adds up to a healthy commission." She started running numbers through her head.

"That doesn't mean I'll get the entire commission," Connie cautioned. "The broker gets his cut. And there will be other fees."

"Still, it will be a large commission," Colleen interjected. "If the condo is worth, say, nine million and if I have figured right, that means your commission will be somewhere in the neighborhood of $500,000."

"Like I said," Connie reiterated, trying to remain cool, "it's too soon to start counting eggs."

"Nevertheless," remarked Colleen. "the priesthood can use the money, so can Gene. He could use some of it to finish our Four-Plex."

Emma fumed, twisting in her chair. "Aren't we forgetting something here," she said, not hiding the bitterness in her voice. "My mom is the one who earned the money—that is, if the sale goes through. Doesn't she have a say in how it's spent?"

Colleen turned to Emma. "You seem to forget. We belong to a united order. After Connie pays her tithing, she should give the balance to Gene who will give it to the Order." Colleen turned towards Gene. "Isn't that right, honey?"

"I'm afraid so," Gene said apologetically. "We live in a community now and that's the rule."

Emma looked at her mother who appeared to be more interested in the yams than the conversation. "Well, it doesn't sound fair," Emma said contemptuously, her disappointment obvious. "What about taxes? How is she supposed to pay tax?"

"The bishop will compute the taxes," Colleen tantalized, "and give back what he thinks the taxes ought to be, along with how much the bishop thinks Gene should keep towards finishing the Four-Plex."

"How nice," replied Emma, her brown eyes firing daggers at Colleen. "Mom, what do you think?"

"I think its silly to even be talking about it when we don't know if the sale will go through," she replied, trying to sound unconcerned. "There will be plenty of time to worry about who gets what—if the sale goes through. I can see I should have kept it to myself until I knew for sure."

The message in Connie's tone of voice was effective. Nothing more was said about money the rest of the day. Each family member, including Emma, shifted to their best behavior hoping to reduce the tension. But that evening, after all the festivities were over and they were back in the privacy of their trailer house, except for Gene who stayed with Colleen, Emma again pursued the subject of money.

"Mom," Emma pleaded, "can we talk about your commission? I know you didn't want to discuss it in front of Colleen. I'm sorry I got nasty, but she really irked me."

Connie settled herself on the couch. "I got tomorrow off and there's no school. What do you say we take Keith and go to a movie?"

"I would like that," Emma replied. "But I would still like to talk about your commission."

"Okay," she relented. "What do you want to know?"

"If you make the sale, are you going to turn your commission over to Daddy so he can give it to the Order?"

"You know," Connie replied with a sigh, "I've been so busy and excited over the possibility of selling the condo that I didn't think once about the group laying claim to my commission. Thanks to Colleen, bless her greedy little heart, I have to face the probability. If the condo closes, it won't be easy handing it over to the priesthood."

"Mom," Emma pleaded, "you don't have to give it to the priesthood."

"I shouldn't have confided in your dad," Connie lamented. "I was so excited about the possibility of making the sale, I had to tell somebody."

"Why didn't you tell me?" Emma asked. "You know I can keep a secret."

"I didn't want to get your hopes up. I wanted to surprise you."

"Mom, you still haven't answered my question," Emma said, fearful of what her mother might say. "Are you going to give the money to the priesthood?"

"I guess I can't give you an answer until the condo closes.

Until then, I don't want to be distracted. I really need to concentrate on the closing."

"They're going to be drooling, you know," predicted Emma. "They can't wait to get their hands on your money. They don't care about you."

"I know," agreed Connie. "It presents a real dilemma ..." She sighed again. "I really love my job. I enjoy the challenge of meeting new people and putting together a sale. I hadn't even thought about the money. I don't know if anyone will believe me, but I didn't go into real estate just for the money." She ran a slender hand and fingers through her long auburn hair.

"I believe you, Mom."

"I know you do." She gave Emma an appreciative smile. "I don't know what I would have done without you these last few months. You've been there when I needed you and I can't tell you how much that meant to me. But for the next few weeks you've got to trust me. I want to put this real estate deal together in the worst way."

"In other words, don't make waves."

"Yes, Darling," she replied, "this deal could mean a lot to me."

"You've got my word, no waves," vowed Emma. "In May I'll be eighteen. When I graduate from high school, I'm out of here."

"And I surely won't stop you."

Gene had been warned that conflict between wives would inevitably occur. Now it had happened and he knew it would not go away, not when money was the issue. During his first ten years of marriage to Connie, the idea that he would ever love another woman was as alien as breathing water. But marriage had become routine. Even though fidelity, love, and respect were never in question, the zest had slowly evaporated.

Studying the mysteries of early Mormonism had added spice to his mundane life. When he became converted to the concept of plural marriage, life became meaningful, exciting, and adventurous again. He stopped drifting from one materialistic fad to another. If Joseph Smith could risk death for the gospel, then Gene finally decided he could risk his reputation, yes, even his church membership.

And then came the burst to his psyche when a young beautiful woman asked to become his plural wife. With new erotic magnetism, he became more productive, intuitive, and virile. But with that also came the responsibility of pleasing two wives. Colleen was an effervescent fountain of optimism and affection. Connie remained conflicted with insecurities and doubts.

At Thanksgiving dinner, Gene had observed Colleen asserting herself, dropping her anchor, establishing her place in the family. In response, Connie had forged her own boundaries. Gene realized he had entered a wilderness that had few paths. He loved both women and desperately wanted peace and unity. But how could he please one without neglecting the other? Gene learned to walk a tightrope.

Gene cherished free agency. He did not believe in managing his wives and children with pious threats of damnation like some polygamists. Both wives were spunky, self-motivated, and not afraid to speak their minds. When conflicts brewed, he kept his fingers crossed hoping they would solve themselves. He learned never to take sides and only addressed problems when they surfaced. He believed in shaping behavior by accentuating the positive and avoiding the negative, and it worked for him with his large office staff.

While Connie made few demands, Colleen had many needs and minor crises, but then would reward Gene with amorous ovations. While this time away robbed Connie, Emma, and Keith of his love and nurturing, Gene did not know how to compensate them other than to express extra love and interest while staying in their trailer, where he was actually grateful for the rest. The trailer became a sanctuary from the incessant chores dreamed up by Colleen.

Gene prayed that his wives would somehow become more harmonious. But when Connie had not responded to Colleen's efforts at friendship, Colleen turned to her own sisters and the wives of her brothers. Preoccupied with her employment, Connie made no close friends in the group, or at least this is the excuse she used.

Gene began to observe the inequities in various families and, from the remarks of some of the younger men, he realized their quest for multiple wives was more erotic than religious. He hoped Emma would not be attracted to one of them. Gene knew the group took the position that their lifestyle was the complete answer to all sociological needs, as well as spiritual. But he wanted Emma to know the thrill of a dozen red roses and a candlelight dinner at a four-star restaurant. He wanted her to be able to wade in the surf of the Atlantic and Pacific and fly to exotic parts of the world. The life of a polygamist was hard and demanding, with endless sacrifices. And he vowed that his wives would not be isolated from the rest of the world. As finances permitted, they would travel, smell the flowers, and sample exotic cuisines.

But then, where would he get the extra money.

Gene confided his innermost thoughts to a friend he had made in the group. Randy was also a corporate executive and had only been in the group two years. Like Connie, Randy's wife had come grudgingly, along with their four children. But unlike Connie, Randy's wife had made a sincere effort to make friends with the new wife, and it seemed to be working.

Gene had long talks with Randy, both to get his frustrations off his chest and to solicit advice. As he watched Randy's family from a distance, he wondered what Randy knew that he did not. But Randy told him nothing he didn't already know, nothing he had not already tried.

And his parents hostility troubled him deeply. They had always been a close family, each of his siblings successful in their own right. Naturally, his parents felt successful ... until Gene made his momentous decision to become a polygamist. They had been aghast. But Gene reasoned that alienation from family was simply one more price he had to pay for his dedication to God, to his own eternal glory.

And Keith ... his pride and joy, his certain-to-be-successful son. Keith's refusal to give the new life a fair chance broke his heart. Yet he knew that free agency applied to everyone, even his own children. He knew Emma felt deeply resentful of Colleen and Gene's time with his new family. Yet he firmly believed that she would come around ... in time. Just as Connie would.

Connie had been even more spiritual than Gene. Her

obedience to her religious beliefs made him proud of her. Surely she would come to see the truth. And he needed her to become more compliant. The priesthood leaders continued to counsel him and even pressure him to be the authority figure in his families. To take charge. To be commanding. In short, to be the man they thought they brought into the group.

Keeping secrets was a new pastime for Gene. Balancing his secret polygamist life with his business world self became a daily labor. Gene could not place Colleen's picture alongside Connie's on his desk, nor could he brag about the new baby coming. Questions about his family life were answered creatively. They knew he had moved and had a new phone number, but they knew little else. What they did know is that Connie no longer called him at work, and neither did his mother.

Whereas Gene had been open and gregarious with his staff, now he became quiet. When quizzed if things were all right at home, he explained that he simply wanted to focus harder on doing a good job for his company.

The other executives suspected he was having an affair. But they said nothing. When Gene was considered along with two other men for a promotion, the vice-president gave it to a newer man. Gene said nothing, and no one in his office said anything. Although still fair in his dealings with them, he was no longer the boss they had come to love and admire.

His former church ward knew he had suddenly moved, but they didn't know why and no one in the family would provide more than vague reasons. No one was sure where they were living and Gene made sure it stayed that way. If he could avoid being excommunicated by the LDS Church, which he surely would be if they discovered he was involved in polygamy, then his secret would be more easily protected.

By law it was illegal and one was open to prosecution. Gene knew that Utah had not pursued polygamists for many years, but that could change.

Chapter Twelve

The group dances were always the same. Nothing ever changed. Even so, the dances were one of the few entertainments enjoyed by the faithful. And it was an opportunity for young girls to discuss the seamy events unfolding in the group, like who's marrying who—who left the group—and who's in trouble with the priesthood. It was also an opportunity to talk about boys—especially the capricious, jaunty boys of the group.

The dances were attended by the same people each month, wearing the same clothes, and with only a smattering of new faces. But it was still the best occasion for young girls to visit and exchange romance stories without worrying about the prying ears of the priesthood matriarchs.

Emma noticed Seth dancing with one of his wives. She had not seen Seth or his wives at the last two dances. She wondered if it was because of the rumor that Seth was under investigation by federal authorities for stock fraud. The rumors alleged his innocence and that he was being persecuted for his religion. But after what Lillian had confided to Emma, it was her guess Seth was probably guilty. Other people in the group had been in trouble with the law, especially the IRS. It was always the same story—they were being persecuted because of their religion.

Emma caught Seth's glancing eye. She pretended not to notice and scanned the dance hall for Lillian. Not finding her and satisfied she was at home, Emma decided to tease Seth by giving him a taste of what he was missing. It was a daring and devilish idea, but she didn't care. It was a grand opportunity to test some of those superior female talents Lillian had talked about at camp.

Emma accepted every dance with the gaiety of a supple nymph, exaggerating her performance when Seth took his turn. She stretched to expand the size of her bosoms, thrust out her compact bottom, and puckered like Marilyn Monroe until Seth's tongue hung on his chin. She enjoyed every minute until Bruce, with baffled astonishment, his Adam's apple jumping up and down asked, "Emma, what's got into you?"

Her face flushed and she was immediately overcome with embarrassment. "Too much starch in my clothes," she lied, fearing she had overdone it. The rest of the night she returned to her old modest self but inwardly was pleased with the effects of the power she possessed.

Mary and Emma were talking when Gwen approached, accompanied by other boys and girls in their clique. Among them were two new faces, one a pretty, dark-haired girl in a gold sweater and brown skirt. Gwen introduced her as Grace.

"Are you new to the group?" asked Emma.

"Not exactly," said Grace. "I'm with the Johnston group but I have friends in this group." With Grace was a tall, slender twenty-year-old. Emma assumed that he too was with the Johnston group but when Gwen introduced him she said he was from the community in Wyoming that was part of the Partridge group. His name was Byron. "I don't have much to do with people in our group anymore," Byron said.

Byron was from the same unpolished mold as Bruce, a misfit more at home on a cattle ranch. And like Bruce he seemed virtuous and hardworking. He shuffled around as the girls talked, uncomfortable in a crowd.

"Me and Byron have been going together," said Grace. "We'd like to get married but it's causing some problems at home. My dad don't like Byron. He wants me to marry someone in our group, an old man with six wives."

"You would be the seventh!" asked Emma.

"Yeah," she replied. "I don't like him. He's too old and no fun, besides I would only see him once a week."

Grace didn't seem bashful or shy about discussing her predicament. As she talked, Byron shuffled and listened attentively as if on guard. He was obviously hopelessly in love and ready to wade rivers or climb mountains in defense of his woman's honor. But Emma began to suspect Grace didn't share his adoration; she acted more like a canary that had slipped its cage, reveling in freedom.

"Tell me about your group," Emma asked Grace. But it was Byron who answered.

"They're more oppressive than our group," said Byron, in a country drawl. "They pretend to be poor but they're really very rich. All they think about is money, how to make it and how to save it. Many women don't even have a refrigerator or stove, or if they do, it's so old it barely works ... and instead of money, the men are paid with little tickets that they can only exchange at one of the Johnston group stores. Old man Johnston died a couple of years ago and now one of his sons is the boss, and is he ever a tyrant. As soon as a girl is old enough to make a baby, she is married off to one of their own people."

Gwen moved over and let Byron sit next to Grace.

"The Johnston boys get first pick of the girls." continued Byron. "Paul Johnston ... he's the leader ... has over thirty wives, all young girls, and Grace says he even delivers his own babies. And his brothers have lots of wives, one has eleven, the other, nine."

Disgust spread across Byron's face and he shook his head. "If you go out in the parking lot you'll see three kids from the Johnston group sittin' in their cars looking for girls. They can't find any girls in their own group because the Johnston boys snag em' all up. So they come over here. They're desperate."

"Why don't they come in?" asked Emma.

"Bashful," said Byron. "The girls know they're out there. A few sneak out and talk to them. That keeps em' coming back."

"So what are you going to do?" asked Emma, directing her question at Grace.

"I'm looking for a place to stay until I can work things out," said Grace.

"If she goes home, her dad will brainwash her," interjected Byron.

Gwen spoke up. "We thought Grace could spend a day or two with each one of us ... you know ... until she and Byron decide what they're going to do."

Both Gwen and Grace looked at Emma hopefully. "We were hoping she could spend a couple of days with you," said Gwen.

All eyes were on her. How could Emma tell them no? How

could she not help Grace escape? Kids wanting out of polygamy had to stick together. It didn't matter what group they were from, they were all in the same predicament, only with Grace it was more severe.

"Of course," said Emma, "she can stay as long as she wants. I know my mother will understand."

Connie did understand but couldn't help worrying about reprisals. "How old are you?" asked Connie.

"I'm eighteen," she replied.

"Then you're old enough to make some decisions about your own life," said Connie. "But to be safe, let's not say anything to our neighbors about where you come from."

Over the years the Johnston cartel had invested wisely in many retail and wholesale ventures: farms, amusement machines, a wholesale restaurant supply, a coal mine, and a huge cattle ranch in Nevada once owned by a movie actor. Dissidents of the group alleged that the Johnston Clan owned as many as one hundred businesses throughout the Intermountain west. Because of their alleged vast wealth, the Johnstons had come under public scrutiny as if it were a sin for fundamentalists to be successful in business. If any of their people got into trouble with the law, the press immediately exploited it.

Even though each polygamist group evolved around the same fundamentalist doctrines, each had its own peculiar characteristics. The Partridge group, for example, attempted to supplant the Mormon Church in every respect, including the giving of heavenly endowments. The Grass Valley people in southern Utah adopted the modest fashions of the twenties and their women were sometimes mistaken for Amish. They believed that plural marriage was all that was necessary to catapult adherents to the celestial kingdom and did not bother with the endowment.

The Johnston group, the most secretive and smallest of the three groups, carried the united order to extreme, and had turned self-imposed privation into a virtue. A few members of their group had been exposed by the news media as living in deplorable, pigsty conditions.

Whenever their group came under attack by the media, it was the policy of their leader, Paul Johnston, a brilliant young man in his late thirties, to turn the other cheek and weather the assault until their enemies lost interest. This policy was enforced even when the accusations of their enemies were blatant lies. Paul Johnston took the position that he should not speak ill of another human being even if that other human being was a slanderer, liar, and cheat.

It was difficult but not impossible to get out of the Johnston group, but nearly impossible to get in. Their growth came from children born and raised among the existing families. By their own figures, they only numbered about a thousand, small in comparison to the Grass Valley and Partridge groups. But small meant greater control. It was an organization where trust in the superiority and nobility of the leader was imperative. Paul was more than a president, or king, he was a general as well and that required adherents to be like soldiers and follow instruction without hesitation.

Grace's father managed three profitable thrift stores. There were not enough Johnston cohorts to fill all his employment needs so Grace's father hired outside their group. Two of these outside employees were Bonnie, a lady in the Partridge group, and her son, Raymond. And Bonnie's daughter had married into the Johnston group.

Grace's father knew of Grace's friendship with Byron. He correctly deduced that Grace would be hiding out with some of Byron's friends. He instructed Raymond, whose loyalty was to his employer, to ferret her out. Raymond proved to be a capable sleuth and reported back to his employer that Grace was staying with Emma.

The father telephoned Connie after failing to located Gene, making his appeal to a mere woman. He assumed that because Connie was a plural wife, she would be sympathetic. It was from the conversation with Grace's father that Connie learned that Grace was already married and the seventh wife of one of the Johnston boys. That night Connie and Emma had a serious talk with Grace.

"Your father told me you're already married," Connie said with concern, but she did not want to alienate Grace. "Why didn't you tell us the truth?"

Grace fidgeted in her seat on the sofa, avoiding Connie's eyes.

Then in a soft, repentant voice she said, "I was afraid if Byron knew I was married he wouldn't like me."

Emma studied Grace all curled up at the end of the sofa, a pillow in her lap for security. Emma couldn't help but feel sorry for her, caught in a lie, but a lie that was easily forgiven considering her predicament. Most girls would have done the same.

"Did you want to marry this man?" Connie asked gently.

"No," she said convincingly. "My dad made me do it. I didn't want to marry him."

"You mean your father forced you?" asked Connie incredulously.

"Not exactly," said Grace. "He just kept telling me what a good man he was ... how lucky I was to marry in a royal linage and how important it would be to our family. He didn't care how I felt. The only thing that mattered to him was having a Johnston as a son-in-law. He'll do *anything* to look good in their eyes."

"I don't know what to say," said Connie. "Your father kept saying he was trying to reunite a family, and he accused Byron of trying to break it up. I really don't want to get in the middle of this. If you're dead set against going back to this man, why don't you go to the police?"

"I don't want to get my dad in trouble," she replied. "If I go to the police ... well ...."

"What about Byron?" asked Emma. "He needs to know you're married."

"I've already told him," said Grace.

"How did he take it?" asked Emma.

"It just made him more determined to get me away from the Johnstons. He wants to go to Nevada and get legally married ... that it would solve everything."

"How do you feel about marrying Byron?" asked Connie.

"I don't know, there's so much to think about," said Grace, "I really like Byron ..." She let her eyes fall to the floor, avoiding Connie's gaze. It was obvious to Connie that Grace was a confused little girl.

"You've got to decide what you're going to do," said Connie. "The state doesn't recognize plural marriage so in their eyes you're a single woman. But I told your father I would try and have both you and Byron call him and maybe set up a meeting."

Grace agreed to telephone her father. Then she confided more. Her husband had sequestered her in a small apartment house, a rundown, dumpy dwelling owned by the cartel. It was a typical arrangement, she said. Young wives were scattered around the valley and given jobs.

In three months Grace had only seen her husband five times. She had not conceived on the wedding night nor during the one day honeymoon—like most young cooperative brides. Pregnant wives were more easy to manage and less likely to roam. Although she worked at one of her father's thrift stores during the day, she was terribly lonely and bored at night with nothing but the television.

Grace grew depressed sitting home alone night after night and craved social interaction with kids her own age. It didn't take long for her cravings to overcome her fidelity. Like other neglected young brides in the Johnston group she decided to sneak out at night. She couldn't romp with the kids in her own group for fear her husband and father would find out, so she looked elsewhere and connected with the kids in the Partridge group.

"I'm not the only girl in our group that snuck out at night looking for fun," Grace told Emma. "I know of one girl my age, she was the eleventh wife, who had a guard. Her husband had an older wife stay with her so she couldn't sneak out. But they couldn't stop her. More than once she climbed out the bathroom window and wouldn't come back till early in the morning. Finally her father took her out of town to a farm where kids are disciplined and beat her senseless."

"My father would never, ever do that," stated Emma

"Well, it happened," said Grace. "I'm not making it up. In our group you do what you're told, or else."

Grace did not sleep at Emma's that night. Byron picked her up and they drove off in his old Ford pickup. It was the last time Emma saw her.

Emma looked forward to Sunday sacrament meeting because she would see Gwen and hear news about Grace and Byron. Their clique always gathered at the southeast corner of the parking lot.

"Mom," Emma said, "I'm going to find Gwen."

Connie was also anxious to hear what had happened to Grace. Appalled at the way young girls were treated in the Johnston group, Connie seriously considered calling the authorities, but then realized, what could the police do unless Grace and the other girls cooperated. She desperately hoped one of the girls would finally get fed up and go to the police.

Several kids gathered around the driver's side of Byron's old pickup, Gwen among them. Byron sat behind the wheel, his jaw hanging on his chest. The expressions of the other kids matched Byron's.

"I don't understand her," Gwen was saying to Byron as Emma walked up. "I thought she wanted her freedom."

Byron shook his head. "So did I. It sure makes me look like a fool."

"What happened?" asked Emma.

Byron raised his head and looked at Emma. "Grace went back."

"But why?" asked Emma.

"I don't know," said Byron. "I went to pick her up and she was gone, didn't leave word or anything. I looked all over. Finally I called her dad. He said she'd gone back to her husband and threatened me if I don't stay away."

"Maybe they kidnaped her," said Gwen.

"That's what I thought," said Byron. "I told her father I didn't believe him, that I was coming to get her … and I was bringing the police. He told me he would have Grace call me and prove it. I said I wanted to talk to her face to face, but he refused. She called back about fifteen minutes later." And then Byron grew silent. He stared at the dashboard of the pickup, his elbow on the steering wheel, his chin resting in his hand.

"What did she say?" asked Gwen. "Was she brainwashed?"

Byron looked up. "No, she wasn't brainwashed. She said she just changed her mind and decided to go back. I could tell by talking to her that she went back on her own."

"Byron," Emma asked. "Did you and Grace call her dad after you left my house?"

"Yeah, we both talked to him. Me first … but all we did was argue." He glanced down at the dashboard. "I told him I wanted to marry her and that it was wrong to force her to marry someone she didn't love. I promised to take good care of her ... but he wouldn't listen."

"What did Grace say?" asked Emma.

"She mostly just listened. After she hung up, she said he told her he would get her a new car at the auto auction, a new refrigerator, and a bunch of other stuff if she would go back to that guy. I think he bribed her back ... and ... I guess she would rather have a new car than me ..."

During the drive home after sacrament meeting, Emma gave the report to her mother.

Connie said, "I think Grace is a very insecure, naive little girl. And clearly she did not have the same affection Byron had for her. Maybe all she needed was a little adventure. Now she's back safe and secure in her little cage, surrounded with expensive gifts. Down deep, I think the reality of earning her own living, making her own decisions, being on her own was too scary for Grace."

"You know what, Mom? I think it's horrible to force your daughter to marry some old man. Dad would never *make* me do that. But, you know, as I've thought about it, maybe Grace would have been unfaithful to Byron too."

"You may be right," said Connie. "Those Johnston people are a strange bunch. I'm glad your dad didn't get mixed up with them. At sacrament meeting I sat next to Bonnie, the mother of that girl that married into the Johnston group. What she told me made me sick.

"I know that not all polygamists are bad, most are just people struggling to make a life, looking for some kind of happiness, even if they think they have to get to heaven to find it," said Connie. "I can see that some are exceptional people. But when I hear these ... horror stories ... it makes me ashamed I'm one of them." Her visage turned bitter with disgust. "Those damned Johnston men and their lies. They'll say anything to manipulate their women."

"What exactly did that lady tell you, Mom?"

"Her daughter who married into the Johnston group has arthritis and her fingers and hands are gnarled and twisted. The poor thing ... she's only in her late twenties. It's all she can do to take care of her children and do the housework. After her husband found another wife, he started treating her like poop. But that's not what makes me so angry." Connie took a deep breath, "If that girl were my daughter I'd scratch his eyes out."

"Mom, what happened!"

"The husband of this girl … and her father-in-law … told her that the reason she suffered from arthritis is because of the wickedness of her mother."

"WHAT!" exclaimed Emma. "You can't be serious."

"Oh, I'm serious all right. They told her that the sins of the mother were being visited upon the daughter. You have to remember, these girls are brought up to accept whatever their menfolk say. Until she talked with her mother she actually believed it. Now she says she knows differently, but she's caught in a dilemma. What is she to do? And, Emma, she has to have nagging doubts about who is right … her mother or her priesthood leaders. What an incredible burden to live with."

"Why do men do that?" Emma said, not really expecting an answer.

"In this case," said Connie. "The husband and father-in-law already had it in for Bonnie. Something happened while she worked for them. I don't know what, but that's why she quit and I'm sure they wanted to get even."

"What I meant," said Emma, "is why do men think they can just say or do whatever they please to women and get away with it?"

"It's lack of respect," said Connie, "they won't allow women to be their equal, almost like they see women as a threat. It's all very complicated. For example, the husband of this girl we're talking about, I am told, will go out of his way to help another man. But where women are concerned he's a rat."

"I heard something else about the Johnston boys," said Emma. "At first I didn't believe it but after what you just told me, now I do."

"And what did you hear?" said Connie.

"On a date, some of the Johnston boys have one thing in mind," said Emma, "to have sex. If they're successful, they tell the girl she will go to hell unless she marries him. It's just another way to get wives. But what makes me really mad … by marrying him, she does end up in hell."

Chapter Thirteen

The new year arrived on a frigid, crisp winter morning when the sun had no power against the arctic air and the mercury plunged ten degrees below zero. Three-foot drifts clogged the community roads. Yard long ice cycles hung from the houses, and extra hay was fed to the cattle to keep them warm. Outside, all was quite except for the roar of a racing snowmobile. Men worried about freezing water pipes. Women busied themselves with cooking and sewing. Kids watched Walt Disney videos. The butane heater in Connie's trailer worked overtime. Emma and Keith dug out wool sweaters and spread extra blankets on the beds. Gene was with Colleen, working on Connie's part of the Four-Plex.

With the new year came the closing of the condo sale. Miraculously, Connie was able to conceal her excitement, but it wasn't easy. Inside she was ready to burst. She had to fight off the impulse to strut down Salt Lake's Main Street with clenched fists held high, yelling "I DID IT!"

But on the surface, she was as indifferent as a poker player. Weeks of hard work had finally paid off. Now what to do with the money? She knew she could no longer escape looking deep into her soul, asking what she really believed to be true, a journey she had tried to avoid for the sake of her family. She had no choice but to evaluate her loyalties and consider what her responsibilities really were. So much was at stake, so much to consider: the priesthood, the Four-Plex, Gene, the children, her own peace of mind and welfare. At first she believed the money would solve problems, but looking at the whole picture objectively, the money had instead created problems. But it had forced her to face herself and what she really believed.

The first few days after the closing were like a dream in which she rehearsed the agony and uncertainty of each minute negotiation, the sudden changes in the contract, the doubts, fears, and finally the closing. It was a week before she told Emma the news. She told Gene nothing.

During that first week Connie consulted a tax man and opened up a savings account and a checking account in a new bank in a suburb of Salt Lake City. And on the day she told Emma, she took the kids shopping, bought them new clothes and dinner at a fancy restaurant. Emma was as excited as her mother. They both giggled and joked like adolescent girls. But with the excitement came the worry and Emma couldn't help wonder what her mother would do with the money? Would she give it to her dad—who would give it to the priesthood?

The waitress brought the check. In a few moments the merriment would be over and they would once again be thrust back into the realities of their world. Emma couldn't stand the suspense any longer.

As calmly as she could manage, she asked, "Mom, what are you going to do with the money?"

Connie was in no hurry to answer. She smiled lovingly and took a last bite of prime rib.

"Oh Momma," she pleaded. "PLEASE don't give it to Daddy. I would rather burn it than have the priesthood get it."

Somehow Connie had to calm Emma's fears without committing herself. She looked into Emma's searching eyes and said, "That money is not going anywhere until I'm finished talking with my tax attorney. In the meantime I'm working on another commercial sale, not as lucrative as the condo, but well worth the time." She turned towards Keith who was scooping up the last spoon of strawberry ice cream. "I don't want our conversation repeated to anyone. Not even your father. Understand?"

Keith shrugged. "Who's to tell? Dad's busy with Colleen. I hardly ever see him and I don't have anything to do with the kids in the group."

"Well, that may change," his mother said. But Keith paid no attention.

Connie had withdrawn from all social activities in the group except for sacrament meeting, using her job as an excuse. The entire community was excited about her potential condo sale and waited patiently for the closing. She knew it would be just a matter of time before the cat was out of the bag. Before that happened, she needed to examine even more deeply her true feelings about the group and the polygamist religion, a lifestyle that demanded everything you owned, including your thoughts, in this life and the next.

Connie had struggled with these issues since she and Gene had entered the group. Just when she thought she understood the workings of a polygamist mind, some new event occurred, or some new emotion would grab her. She never knew what to expect. It was like someone was watching every move she made. Now, with her sizable commission, she had to find some answers. It's amazing, she mused, how easily money can deflect one's course in life.

She sought out a man named Roger who had walked out on the Partridge group ten years prior. Roger was an outspoken critic against the leadership of the group. Richard Partridge and apostles hated Roger and portrayed him as the archetypical villain of the priesthood. After ten years the people in the group still talked about him as if he were the devil incarnate and cautioned loyal followers to shun him and not listen to his slanders.

Connie expected to see an old man with scraggly hair and wild eyes. What she saw was the opposite, a courteous man in his fifties, bald with a ring of graying hair, a thick mustache and a trim muscular body. He lived in an older remodeled home with all the latest appliances and decor. He invited Connie in. There were several small children playing in the house. "These are my grandchildren," he volunteered.

Roger herded the children into the television room and escorted Connie into the living room where they could talk. A bespectacled, comely blonde lady in her early fifties poked her head into the living room and said cheerfully, "Hi, I'm Helen." It was Roger's wife. She left just as abruptly. Company to Helen was a routine occurrence in their house. Over the last few years there had been dozens of inquiring minds seeking information about the Partridge group and polygamy in general. Helen had hosted state and federal investigators, newspaper and television reporters, and many potential converts, irate relatives of converts, and those like

Connie with second thoughts. Helen returned with a pot of steaming Jasmine tea and cookies.

Connie scanned the room as Helen poured the tea. It had a definite woman's touch. Photographs were plentiful but they were of children and grandchildren.

There was an elegant china closet with pink flowered dishes, gold rimmed bowls, figurines of cherubs, and delicate porcelain blue birds and bunny rabbits. In examining the books in the book case she saw the Bible, many novels written by well known authors, and a few biographies and autobiographies by notable authors. Two oil landscapes hung on the wall, one painted by Walden, a local artist of the early twenties.

"What can I do for you?" asked Roger. His face had a natural pink flush. He was clean shaven except for the mustache and dressed in brown slacks and a plaid shirt, his sleeves rolled up exposing strong hairy arms.

Connie discerned in his face that he knew why she was there so she gave no explanation and came right to the point, "Why did you leave the Partridge group?"

His smile was disarming and non-threatening. He leaned back in the recliner and when he spoke it was with a tone of neutrality. Clearly he was not trying to persuade or win an ally. She could believe or not believe.

"Most people," he began, "conclude that I must have been maligned, slandered or otherwise mistreated and that's why I left. But the truth is I was treated kindly and with respect by the leaders. I left when I discovered that Richard Partridge and two of his henchmen had stolen a large sum of money from a lady in southern Utah. I approached Partridge and asked him if he knew anything about the theft. He lied and said he didn't. A few weeks later I approached him again and showed him conclusive evidence that he had lied and that he was in fact deeply involved in the theft. He did not deny it. He couldn't, the evidence was overwhelming."

Roger looked for some reaction from Connie but found none.

"I asked myself, Is there more about the leadership of this group that I should know about. So a friend and I started digging and we found the leadership was steeped in corruption. Wives were given and taken on whims. Men were inveigled into consecrating their property to the priesthood. I interviewed one man who said he was told the priesthood would make him the steward over his consecrated property, but a month after signing the Quit Claim Deed, he was kicked off.[6] I found that the group was more political than spiritual and they simply used religion as a tool to gain wealth and power. In essence, they were merchandising faith, salvation, and plural wives. The topper was the non-profit corporation that is supposed to own the priesthood property. Members who build on the property are compelled to sign an occupancy agreement. Whoever invented and wrote that document must have been inspired by Joseph Stalin."

At the mention of the occupancy agreement, Connie's heart took a tumble, but she did not let on. She let Roger talk.

"Most of the people in the group are hard working, honest families that would never do what their leaders do. They hear rumors of misdeeds by their leaders but like me, when I was associated with the group, they are busy earning a living and managing their families, and don't really know what's going on behind closed doors." He hesitated and then said, "Nor do they know how their tithing money is spent. Well, I didn't like what I found, especially how the priesthood was using the people's money. It did not conform with my conception of Christianity, so I told Mr. Partridge, 'in all good conscience I cannot sit in sacrament meeting and look at you sitting on the stage knowing that you and others in this group are thieves.' I also told him I had learned that lumber had been removed from their different construction sites to build homes for the priesthood elite on a ranch in the west desert, and that money was skimmed from the company to purchase an expensive irrigation system for the ranch, all illegal activities. I told him good-bye and haven't been back."

"I am told you go out of your way to cause trouble for the priesthood," said Connie, trying not to be argumentative. "One member of the council said you are out to destroy them."

Roger laughed. "I know what they're saying. I also know that in their prayer circles they have cursed me and asked God to eliminate me. Not because I walked out on the group, but because I have helped the lady who was victimized by Partridge and his henchmen. I found her an attorney and provided her with the evidence to file a civil law suit. It is a long convoluted story. Since then, Partridge and his priesthood have done all they can to discredit me and the lady."

"I know they don't like you," said Connie. "But I haven't heard anything about the lady you're talking about. But, I'm not very active socially."

"Well," said Roger, "they circulated one story that she consecrated the money and wanted it back. A consecration is like tithing, a gift, and you can't get it back. Then they started another rumor that claimed she was a prostitute, as if it was okay to steal from a prostitute, but none of the stories are true."

"Aren't you afraid Richard will send someone after you?" asked Connie, her voice registering honest concern.

"If I had exposed criminal conduct during the 1800s, they might have sent Bill Hickman or Porter Rockwell to deal with me, but those days are long gone. So they do the next best thing, they assassinate my character."

Connie nibbled on a cookie and sipped some tea, then asked, "If it's as bad in the group as you say, why aren't people leaving?"

"They are," he replied with a smile. "They come and go like a revolving door. The ones who stay do so because of a symbiotic relationship. The leaders hunger for someone to lead, and the people long to be led. They need each other. The group—no, not the group—the priesthood—it becomes the conscience of the people. And the people are content to let Richard Partridge and the priesthood do their thinking, not only in spiritual matters, but in temporal matters as well."

"Are you suggesting," said Connie, "that people in the group willingly give up their independence?"

"Yes, I am. You see, the individual person shares in what they perceive as the great mission of the group. It provides the true believer purpose and identity in an otherwise mundane life. He feels part of a great cause and it boosts his self- esteem. By living plural marriage he feels elevated above the average man, part of a secret society living higher laws. Besides, it's an exciting adventure. Polygamists are doing something daring, felonious, and sacrificial. But there is more," Roger said, picking up a cookie and washing it down with tea.

"Men have the illusion of power, but their power extends only over their wives and children unless they are part of the group hierarchy. With women, security and religion are the chief motivators and often little else. But even then the security of knowing you will be exalted and always have a roof over your head may be only an illusion. Equality in the group is probably the greatest illusion of all. The group is a despotic organization. The people refuse to believe it, but the priesthood was not formed to serve the people, the people were gathered to serve the priesthood. Each individual is expendable. The people give their allegiance, their talents, their money, their daughters, and sometimes their wives to the priesthood. And in exchange for what? Hope for a higher place in heaven, provided they don't screw up and piss off the priesthood. In all of history there has never been a fair autocratic regime and Partridge's polygamist sect is no exception. I defy any historian to prove me false."

"What does Brother Partridge do with the tithing money?"

Roger chuckled. "Anything he wants. Tithing is a donation, free and clear, no strings. The Corporation of the Presiding Elder of the Apostles of Jesus Christ is a 'sole' corporation. That means Richard Partridge automatically becomes the trustee-in-trust of all the money and property and is accountable only to God. If Partridge is the only one who communicates with God, then in essence, he is God. Ten years ago when I left the group and started exposing some of the corruption, Partridge had exclusive control over the purse strings of the group. He accounted to no member. Since then he has authorized a committee to study and dispose of the tithing money, subject of course to his approval. I was able to obtain copies of minutes of this committee and if the minutes are correct, most of the tithing money goes to speculative building projects controlled by elite members of the group, or get-rich-quick schemes, or to bail the blue-bloods out of bankruptcy. Over the years the priesthood has squandered millions of dollars of people's hard earned money."

"Why don't the people do something about it?" asked Connie. "How can they just sit by and let the priesthood waste their money?"

"That's easy to answer," replied Roger with a smirk. "If you read the Doctrine & Covenants, it is the people's responsibility to pay their tithes. After that, it's none of their business. In other words, the people are commanded to pay a tithe and it is the priesthood's option how to spend it. I asked a fellow once, 'why give them your money when you know they're just going to piss it away?' He said, 'If the priesthood pisses it away they will have to answer to God. I still get my blessings because I'm commanded to pay my tithing. So it really doesn't matter what they do with the money.'"

Connie sighed. "The group isn't going to change, is it?"

"No," answered Roger glumly, "not without pressure from the people, and I don't see that happening. You know, when the United States Government forced Utah to suspend polygamy, the prophet Wilford Woodruff said a revelation had been received from God to abandon polygamy here on the earth, and it was the smartest thing the church ever did. Just look at what the Mormon church is today; it's a powerful international force, and that couldn't have happened the way they were going.

"But I don't see that happening with the fundamentalists. There are a slew of self-appointed prophets, each with his own special illusion, and they all compete with each other for power and tithing money."

"Just one last question," said Connie. "What about the celestial kingdom? Don't you believe that plural marriage is the only way to the celestial kingdom?"

"Traditional Mormons believe that plural marriage will be lived in heaven. And maybe it will be. But do you see a loving, wise God condoning what is going on in the polygamist groups today? And maybe that is why Wilford Woodruff did what he did, because the abuses began occurring even back then. There's lots of literature from those times suggesting it was problematic. Maybe men were the same then, some righteous and others who simply did not know how to handle it."

Connie could see Roger felt very strongly about what he was saying as the tempo in his voice raised.

"From my viewpoint," Roger said, "the Mormon fundamentalist illusion is the perfect scam. And the amazing part of the whole scam is that it is protected by the Constitution. At the present time there are no less than five prophets in Utah all claiming the same authority. They are all collecting the people's tithing, sealing plural marriages, and making the same celestial promises. If the Doctrine & Covenants is true, then only one man can hold the keys of authority at a time. That means that most or all of them are phony. Yet, they are all protected under the First Amendment, freedom of religion and freedom of speech." Roger laughed deep in his throat. "It could only happen in the United States. I guess that's the price of freedom. In a society like ours we have more crime and corruption than in most totalitarian governments. That is the downside of our system. All we can do is try to help each other and try to educate the good men and women preyed upon by imposters like Richard Partridge and his buddies. That's why I speak out against the priesthood leadership of the organized polygamy groups.

"I'm not here to argue for or against the legitimate doctrine of any law abiding church. My position is simply that I am strongly opposed to the abuse and manipulation of good people."

Chapter Fourteen

Graduation was four months away and as each day passed the girls' excitement mounted. Their future was the grand topic. But the future depended upon adequate employment because without jobs and money there could be no future. They needed an automobile for transportation. They needed an apartment. And that was just the beginning. They needed tuition for college.

It was so much fun, and a little scary, to talk about all the things they were going to do. Where they were going to live, what city, what part of town? Even though they knew there were more jobs available around Provo and Salt Lake, they planned to visit the campus of each university and college from Dixie College at the bottom of the state to Utah State University at the top.

All three girls were A students and would soon be applying for scholarships. Mary favored nursing. She loved children and thought it would be great to work in pediatrics. Gwen was the most convivial and gregarious of the three. She didn't have the slightest idea what vocation she might want to enter or even if she wanted one. It was her objective to attend the university where she would meet the right people and the most promising men. She would major in sophistication, how to dress, behave, and converse in a well-bred fashion. Once there she would let nature take its course.

Emma laughed at Gwen's antics, knowing that of the three, Gwen was the best equipped for success. With her sharp wit and sensual beauty, the world was her stage. Gwen loved to party and when it came to the opposite sex, men were defenseless in her capable hands. She had jogged off her surplus pounds and was now a trim, gorgeous eighteen-year-old Cleopatra going on twenty-three. All she had to do was choose wisely.

Emma kept her femininity in reserve. Her prime interest was journalism. Feedback and encouragement from her English literature teacher validated her self-confidence and desire. She knew she had what it takes. She would make journalism her college major, and would seek part-time employment at one of the daily newspapers, it didn't matter which one, as long as she was where she could learn the publishing and writing business. Meanwhile, she spent all her free time inventing and writing short stories, and writing in her journal.

Her journal. Her private, secret journal. A collection of ideas, ambitions, frustrations, loves and fears, and daily events. The journal was Emma's best pal, the nonjudgmental confidante that could always be trusted. Like Keith's pet cocker spaniel, it was always there, understanding, waiting, loving. And if Emma missed more than two consecutive days without making an entry, the journal gently reprimanded her.

In that relaxed state of rich productivity, she and her journal solved all sorts of dilemmas, especially where polygamy was concerned. She asked herself, "Emma, are you being fair? Isn't it true that many decent people enter polygamous relationships for the sake of eternal life and not sexual gratification? Are you letting your feelings for your father and what has happened to your mother blind you?" She reflected deeply. *No, absolutely not.* What I am doing is tearing away the *camouflage* of their religion. Once the netting, branches, and leaves of deception are removed all that seems to remain is lust—lust of wealth, power, and an endless supply of compliant virgins.

That's what she saw and felt. She couldn't help it. Almost without exception, at every sacrament meeting she felt the prying, disrobing eyes of men behind her, beside her, and ogling down from the balcony. Once she was called to the stand to bear her testimony. As she scurried up to the stage she felt like she was walking a gauntlet of probing eyes. She thought of Lillian, how accurately she had diagnosed the sensual frailties of men.

All this and more Emma recorded in her journal. But in the short stories she submitted to her English teacher and shared with school friends, polygamy was never mentioned.

After the dance, Mary spent Saturday night with Emma. The next morning, over scrambled eggs, bacon, fried potatoes, orange juice, and toast, they discussed their future prospects.

Mary said, "Did you hear Gwen say she thought she landed a summer job as a hostess in the restaurant of that new deluxe hotel in Salt Lake?"

"Yeah," answered Emma. "I hope she gets it. She'd be good. But what about you, Mary? We've got to find you a job, something you'd like."

Mary squirmed in her chair. "I know. I've been thinking about it. I'd really like a job working with children in a hospital."

"Once you get your nursing degree you'll have it made," said Emma. "But until then, we got to find you something that pays good."

Mary was the most brainy of the three, also the most withdrawn and lacking in social skills. What she needed, Gwen and Emma decided, was a job with friendly surroundings where she could meet and deal with the public. The perfect place was Lillian's dress shop. Mary would not only learn to meet the public but learn the current fashions, how to dress, and how to develop her talents and beauty. But Mary was leery, uncertain of her abilities. In the classroom she was confident and composed, but working in a sophisticated dress shop was like leaping from root beer to champagne.

"You would be perfect for the job," said Emma excitedly. "If I can't get on with a newspaper, I'm going to ask Lillian for a job too."

Doubt masked Mary's face.

"Look at it this way," said Emma. "You'd have your choice of all those beautiful dresses … not to mention the cosmetics. You could learn the latest fashions and then teach me and Gwen. You'd be a knockout."

A grin spread across Mary's face. "Me, a knockout?"

"Sure," said Emma. She reached over and with her hand pushed Mary's long blonde hair up on top of her head and swirled it around. "With your figure you could wear anything and look magnificent. You would be the sultry type, dripping with charm and sensuality, modeling your own dresses. The men would go mad with desire, the women green with envy." Mary pursed her lips and gazed haughtily over her nose at imaginary admirers. And they both giggled.

111

"I mean it," said Emma. "I'll even go with you to see Lillian."

"Do you really think I would be good at selling dresses?" she asked.

"Think? I know you'd be good," assured Emma.

"I don't know," said Mary. "If I came home all painted up wearing one of those slinky dresses, my mom would chase me out of the house."

"Hey," said Emma. "Have you forgotten? We'll have an apartment of our own. You can wear whatever you want. And if you get the job before we have our own apartment, I know Lillian will let you change at the shop."

Mary hesitated, biting her lower lip, weighing the pros and cons. Emma empathized with Mary, discerning Mary's struggle to overcome feelings of inadequacy. Emma knew that Mary's apprehension was not a personality defect, but the results of lifelong subtle programming. Mary and hundreds of children like her had been conditioned to be emotionally and socially dependent upon the priesthood. In the group Mary was firm and secure. She knew how to behave, what was expected—she knew all the acceptable colloquial words and phrases. But outside the group, in the gentile world called Babylon, Mary was an alien, a shy stranger in an evil, godless society. She had been brought up to see only one side of life, the priesthood side. As long as she conformed to the priesthood blueprint she was safe and secure, to venture beyond the boundary was sheer folly and dangerous.

The intellectual part of Mary rebelled against priesthood domination and the confining doctrines. But in direct opposition to her desire for liberty and independence, her subconscious sent ominous messages—you don't fit in, the gentiles won't like you, they'll make fun of you, they don't understand you, they will cheat you, they will hurt you—and you will fail.

Mary stopped chewing on her lower lip and looking at Emma once again, "Do you really think I could sell dresses?"

Emma knew what she really meant was, "Do you think I can really adapt to the ways of the gentile without feeling guilty?" She smiled reassuringly at Mary. "I'm positive. You are the most intelligent girl I know. You can do anything you set your mind to."

Emma and Gwen helped Mary sort through the racks of

dresses while they waited for Lillian who was busy with a factory rep. They positioned Mary in front of the mirror and held up dress after dress until she picked out a blue, yellow, and gray print. Then they coerced her into trying it on. It fit snugly, complementing the curvatures of her trim torso and then daintily cascaded over her hips, the hem ending half way between her ankles and knees. While Emma combed Mary's hair into a ponytail, Gwen dabbed lipstick, mascara, and eye shadow across her blushing face. When they were done, they turned her around so she faced the mirror—she was gorgeous. Gwen and Emma took turns hugging her.

From behind them came a woman's voice. "Who's the foxy lady?" It was Lillian. Mary beamed and gave Lillian a big appreciative hug.

"That's your new saleslady," answered Emma proudly. Unbeknownst to Mary, Emma had already approached Lillian with the idea of hiring Mary. It so happened that Lillian expected to need a part-time employee by June and agreed. Lillian's sister-wife was having complications with her pregnancy and planed to quit the end of May.

"I hope you're serious," said Lillian, "because I'm looking for help."

Mary was flabbergasted. She had worried and worried about approaching Lillian and being turned down, and it happened just like Emma predicted, so easy. It was another excuse for the girls to squeal and hug.

"I'm on my way to have lunch with a friend," said Lillian. "Why don't you girls come along?" She looked at Mary. "We can talk about the job."

"I don't know," said Mary reluctantly. "We ought not impose."

"Nonsense," replied Lillian. "My friend will be delighted. She loves to meet new people."

They all piled into Lillian's Jeep Cherokee.

The restaurant was an extravagant soup and salad emporium. The customers walked along a forty foot food bar with sixty vegetable and fruit selections on either side, everything from red kidney beans to green olives.

Lillian's friend, Jan, was waiting in the lobby. After the introductions, the girls took their time sauntering down the food bar sampling everything that looked yummy until their plates resembled miniature mountains.

Jan was older then Lillian, in her mid-forties, taller, with shoulder length dark hair and a willowy, athletic build. She wore blue slacks and a blue blouse and when she walked, it was with long deliberate strides. But what she lacked in physical femininity, she made up in brains and speech.

Precocious Gwen asked, "Are you with the group?"

"No," answered Jan, "I'm an independent. I don't endorse any group but try to stay friendly with all groups—I like to keep tabs on what's going on."

Lillian spoke up. "Jan is one of those ladies in fundamentalism that thinks for herself. That's why we're such good friends. We don't just flow with the crowd. If something needs doing we do it, and we don't need permission or the blessings of a priesthood to know what is right and wrong."

"It sounds like you're my kind of woman," said Gwen.

"Thanks," said Jan. "Have you heard of the Equal Rights for Polygamist Women movement, ERPW."

Gwen said no. Mary and Emma shook their heads.

"It's a group of polygamist women," said Jan, "who have organized to rebut the bad publicity polygamy has been getting lately. You've probably read in the newspapers where a polygamist man was arrested and convicted for having sex with his niece, and the father of the same girl was arrested and convicted for beating her with a belt for rebelling against her husband, which also happened to be his brother. We don't approve of those kinds of relationships. Unfortunately, those incidents, fueled by bitter polygamist wives, have led the public to believe all polygamist men are abusers and all polygamist women are sexual slaves. It is our goal to change that image and show that polygamy is a mutual religious relationship that should be protected by the constitution under Freedom of Religion and Freedom of Equal Protection."

"Are you in charge of the ERPW?" asked Mary.

"Not exactly, I'm close friends with the ladies who are, and I provide them with valuable information and advice. In that way

I'm very active, but I don't appear at their demonstrations or media interviews. You see, I'm in a unique situation. I'm still a member of the Mormon Church and it would not be wise at this time for me to go public. So I kind of stay behind the scenes as an adviser."

Jan took several bites from her salad and then continued. "I have been associated with the fundamentalist movement for about thirty years and probably know as much about what is going on as anyone."

"From what you say," said Gwen, "I can't tell if you are a polygamist or not."

Jan smiled. "Well, I kind-of am. In doctrine and spirit I definitely am." She squirmed in her chair. "Let me explain. For over twenty years I was, let's say, associated with a man in a fundamentalist relationship. He is an excellent historian and compiler, and a great guy. Between the two of us we published dozens of old journals and essays documenting key fundamentalist subjects. My friend is recognized as an expert on fundamentalism and has testified in court several times, and has been interviewed worldwide. Of course, I was behind the scenes, doing the typing, the editing, making him look good."

"I take it you're no longer associated with this friend," stated Emma.

"That's right," admitted Jan, "I kind of outgrew him ... although we're still friends."

"Tell them what you're doing now," said Lillian.

Jan stared blankly at Lillian, pondering the request, unsure if she should reveal her current project. She surveyed the faces of the girls—bright, intelligent, nonjudgmental, friends of Lillian, fellow freethinkers. It should be all right—and it would be an opportunity to demonstrate the importance of her position, and maybe she could recruit these plucky young girls to her cause.

"I'm working intimately with a Utah state legislator who is sympathetic with the fundamentalist cause. That's not for public distribution," she prefaced. "I am very impressed with this man. He knows how to exercise power and is very dynamic in the delivery of his position. He's a true statesman. This man wants to decriminalize the state laws against polygamy and compel the

State of Utah to apologize for the past persecutions of polygamists. He has traveled the State from one end to the other contacting the leaders of the various groups, rallying them around him. If he is reelected, I'm going to help him accomplish his objectives."

"How you going to do that?" asked Gwen.

"Along with two other polygamist ladies, who incidently are also close friends to this legislator, we are writing a book. It's a compilation of testimonies and antidotes by polygamist women throughout the State telling the virtues and positive attributes of polygamy. We plan to present each senator and representative in the legislature with a copy of the book a week prior to our representative introducing a bill to decriminalize polygamy."

"But aren't the women who submitted testimonies for the book afraid of being exposed?" asked Emma.

"Nope, most submissions have been made anonymously for their protection, or they use a pseudonym. We explain all that in our book."

"Will anonymous contributions affect the credibility of the book?" asked Gwen.

"I don't think so. Nor does our legislator. We're hoping it will help emphasize the need to unveil the cloak of secrecy for honest, devout polygamists. Our ultimate goal is to eliminate the criminal stigma attached to the State Constitution that says 'polygamy shall be forever banned.' As you know, banning polygamy was a condition of statehood. Once the criminal statute has been decriminalized, then, and only then, can honest, productive polygamists integrate with society on an equal footing."

Jan paused again, wondering if these young girls could be trusted. The information she had was dynamite. If it leaked to the wrong people it could upset their entire strategy. But there again, they needed followers, strong young women not afraid to stand up for the rights of women. Women with the guts to do what the men had been afraid to do. Women with vision, intelligence, and the power of discernment to select the right man for the right job, knowledgeable men who realize women are good for more than bearing children. The Movement needed women with brains that could pick and support men who would make a place for women in the theocracy. After all, a polygamist man is nothing without the woman. So he must either totally subject the woman or allow her to share in the decision making. Jan thought it was time to force total subjection of women into the past.

Women had proven over and over again they are more wise than men. Women are not caught up in the petty jealousies over priesthood authority and can relate intelligently between groups. Her movement would ultimately result in the emancipation of all women and unite them in the pursuit of common objectives. The men could bicker over priesthood keys, but once the polygamist women realized that the power of the priesthood rests not in heaven but in their laps, the power base would shift from the men to the women, and Mormon fundamentalism would be much better off.

Emma was flabbergasted. Jan was obviously a very bright lady, as well as very ambitious. How could she go along with something that ridiculous … unless she had a personal agenda. The more she learned about Mormon fundamentalism, the more she believed it was all about power. Simply being a good Christian was just a little part of the fundamentalist lifestyle. Emma kept her thoughts to herself. It wouldn't do to offend Jan and embarrass Lillian.

On the way back to the dress shop, Emma asked Lillian, "What did Jan mean when she said she outgrew her first relationship?"

Lillian laughed. "It meant he took a plural wife without her approval. That's what I like about Jan. She has her own ideas about how things should be done. Unlike most fundamentalist women, Jan is economically secure and materially independent. So if things don't meet with her approval, she can move on."

Mary was unusually quiet on their drive home. Troubled by what Jan had said, Mary's deep desire to leave the group was now mixed with little nagging doubts. Laying in bed at night, she began to ponder if the end was actually upon them, and if polygamy would finally dominate the world as predicted by Partridge. And if her leaving the group would leave her behind in the world of Babylon, with no one to resurrect her if she died, and finally no one to introduce her to Jesus Christ when the time came.

Chapter Fifteen

Gene and Colleen had planned a large family dinner at Colleen's after sacrament meeting. Gene had invited Don from the council and two of his wives. Gene and Don had become more than friendly in the last three weeks.

Don was an entrepreneur specializing in commercial building developments. He had a wonderful new development in mind, a seniors retirement home located near a small town in the mountains east of Salt Lake. It would involve a thirty-acre tract to be developed in three segments over a five-year period. Don produced an attractive artist's sketch of the project and boasted that the project could not fail because the priesthood was investing a goodly sum. Don suggested that if Gene quit his job, they could go into business together. Gene was very flattered by the proposal.

It was 7:30 before they sat down to eat. The rump roast was slightly overdone but everybody pretended not to notice. It had not scorched the precious drippings that were used in the brown gravy. Besides mashed potatoes, Colleen had prepared corn-on-the-cob, an imported out-of-season vegetable. The golden kernels brightened up the table like flowers on a wintery day. She hoped it would impress Don.

Keith took one bite of his corn and blurted, "It's tough."

"Then don't eat it," snapped Colleen.

Keith was about to say something in return but stopped when his mother placed her hand on his. Gene, hoping to avoid a scene said, "That's because the corn was shipped in, probably from Mexico. It loses its taste while in transit. Nevertheless, we should be grateful for having corn-on-the-cob in the winter. Put more butter and salt on it and it will taste just fine."

Emma glanced at Don's two wives. Fay, the youngest of Don's five wives and six months pregnant with her second child, was only a few years older than Emma. Born and reared in the group, she was the youngest daughter of the president of the high priest quorum and was a very shy girl. Her older sister was also married to Don.

Karen was Don's first and head wife and the daughter of Dangerous Dan. She had many of the same outspoken, opinionated characteristics of her father. She could speak authoritatively on any subject and was a devout defender of the priesthood. Having a father and a husband on the council gave her extraordinary credibility and prominence, so much so that she felt comfortable in counseling women of lesser nobility and even men. She was never without strong conviction and had a peculiar habit and remarkable ability to turn around any subject so that it focused on her and her wisdom. In a pinch, she could always validate her polemics with "thus saith the priesthood."

The two men chatted with enthusiasm about the expected success and huge profits from Don's senior citizen project until halfway through dinner when Colleen asked Connie, "Has your sale closed yet?" Gene and Don, as if on cue, stopped talking, waiting for Connie's answer.

Emma swallowed and braced for her mother's answer. Connie had not spoken another word about the sale since the night she took Emma and Keith to dinner and shared her excitement. Emma had kept her mother's secret but still didn't know what her mother intended to do with the money.

Mom, please don't give it away.

Connie knew it was coming and was surprised it had taken this long for Colleen or Gene to ask. Trust Colleen to break the ice, she thought, especially while they had company.

Emma did not hide her anticipation. She turned in her chair so she faced her mother. All eyes were on Connie, even Keith sensed something serious was about to happen.

"It has," said Connie casually and went on eating.

Emma was proud of her mother, her composure was splendid, her demeanor aloof and controlled.

"How long ago?" asked Colleen.

"Two weeks."

Colleen was aghast. With just enough sarcasm to make her

point, she glanced first at Gene for effect and then back at Connie, saying, "And you're only telling us now?"

Connie ignored the question.

"So how much was your commission?" asked Colleen, behaving as if she had just uncovered a terrible conspiracy.

"Not as much as everyone hoped," replied Connie, unperturbed.

Colleen felt the rebuff and turned to Gene for help but Gene, uneasy about the interrogation, was studying Connie hoping she would give him a clue how to proceed. Unable to check her impatience, Colleen asked, "Just how much did you get?"

"That's personal," answered Connie, still maintaining her cool.

"What do you mean personal?" Colleen challenged. "This is a family, you know, we're supposed to share. Have you forgotten?"

"No, I haven't forgotten," said Connie calmly. "I'm just not sure sharing is in my best interest, or the interest of my children."

YEA, MOTHER! She wanted to stand up and cheer. She looked at Colleen whose face had changed from shock to frustration. Don was waiting for the confrontation to unravel. Fay was still lost in her little world. Karen was shifting back and forth on her fleshy hips waiting for an opportunity to enter the fray.

"What about your tithing? Surely you intend to pay your tithing?"

"Not until I have had a chance to discuss it with Gene," answered Connie.

"You've had two weeks to discuss it with Gene," retaliated Colleen. "So talk to him now so we all know what we can count on."

"In private, Colleen," said Connie, raising her voice slightly for emphasis. "This is between me, Gene, and my children. When Gene can find time to come to my trailer we'll discuss it. You can hear my decision from him."

Karen spoke up. "May I offer a suggestion … "

Connie politely but forcefully cut her off. "No, you may not." She pushed away from the table and stood up. "Thank you for a wonderful dinner, Colleen," she said cheerfully. "Come on kids, it's time to go home."

Fifteen minutes after Connie and the kids arrived home in their trailer house, the front door burst open and in stomped Gene. "What on earth has gotten in to you, Connie?"

Connie ignored the question and walked over to Keith and said gently, "Your dad and I need to talk. Would you please wait in your room?" Keith left without argument.

"Maybe you'd better go to your room too, Emma," said Gene sarcastically.

"Emma's old enough to stay," corrected Connie. "What we have to say will involve her also."

Gene ignored the rebuke. "You embarrassed me in front of Don," Gene accused. "How could you? Now he'll think I can't control my wife."

"Well," answered Connie, "if he thinks that, then he's right, you don't control me. I'm supposed to be your helpmate, not your servant." Connie didn't raise her voice but the implication was there. She was no longer the subservient obedient wife. She was going to do her own thinking about her own money.

"You know what I mean," said Gene tempering his anger. He had never seen Connie this defiant and it startled him. Bullying her, he wisely surmised, would get him nowhere. "How big was your commission and why didn't you tell me before now?" he demanded, but with less fury.

Connie looked him directly in the eyes. "I didn't tell you because I didn't want it spread all over the group before I could work out a few things in my mind."

"Like what?"

"Like Emma and Keith's college education."

Gene sighed and plopped himself in a chair. How could he argue against that. What parents in their right minds with a surplus of money wouldn't put some aside for their children's education? Yet, he *had* to object. He was a polygamist now and priorities change. Besides, he had a reputation to think about. Connie had never rebelled like this. And he had never confronted a situation like this before, where he had to take money earned by his wife and give it to a priesthood organization. There was no manual explaining where to begin or how to proceed. He was on his own.

Emma watched silently. Her parents were so absorbed in their confrontation that they had forgotten she was there. And this was the first time she had ever witnessed a heated argument between them, and it hurt. Until Colleen came into the family there had been almost perfect harmony.

"Surely you're going to pay your tithing?" said Gene. Of the two of them, Connie had the stronger testimony of the law of tithing. So Gene concluded tithing would be a good place to start talking some sense into her. Before Connie could answer, there was a knock at the door.

"Now who could that be?" said Gene perturbed by the interruption.

Emma thought, *Probably Colleen and that nosey wife of Don's*.

Gene opened the door and in stepped apostle Dangerous Dan. Don was right behind him. Dan stood just inside the door flashing his Cheshire-cat grin. Don nudged around him rubbing his hands together. "Boy, it's cold out there." Then he looked at Connie apologetically and said, "I hope you will forgive us for intruding, but we're here in behalf of the Lord."

Emma rolled her eyes.

Dangerous Dan put away his catty grin, his lower lip protruded resolutely as he shifted smoothly into a serious mode. He grabbed Gene's right hand and pumped it vigorously and while resting his left hand on Gene's shoulder said heartily, "Good evening, dear Brother. I come to you tonight with love and compassion. I was sitting comfortably at home after a refreshing meal thumbing through the Book of Mormon when the spirit came upon me and said that you and your lovely wife were in need of God's counsel. I immediately grabbed my coat and without even saying good-bye to my wife, left my warm home and made a beeline for Colleen's house thinking I would find you there. When I arrived, Brother Don was just leaving. With much reluctance on his part and only because of my bold insistence, he told me what happened, and then I knew the purpose of my mission." He turned towards Connie. "May we sit down, dear Sister?"

Connie pointed to the couch. Both Dan and Don made themselves comfortable. The demeanor of both men was extremely formal and righteous.

"I don't mean to offend you, Brother Dan," said Connie

politely, "but this is a private family matter."

"I understand," said Dan. "But nothing is private from the Lord. As humble servants of the Almighty we are here to help. Now, I understand you have come into possession of a sum of money and you are at an impasse as to what to do. Is that correct?"

"Like I said before, it's a private family matter."

"Dear Sister," said Dan, "the money is unimportant. That's not why we're here. Our mission is about your salvation, your eternal life. That means very much to us. There is a place reserved for you in the celestial kingdom. Don't give it up. I implore you, dear Sister, don't give it up."

Emma thought she was going to vomit. Apostle Dan was so sure of himself. Even she could see through his pious pretensions. She studied her mother's face. It was like stone, revealing nothing. Connie was the only one standing. She gazed down at Apostles Dan and Don, her back straight as an arrow, her countenance regal and stolid, unintimidated by the presence of the two apostles. This was an image of her mother Emma had not seen before and was a little frightening. But as she watched, the more she understood. Her mother was a woman backed into a corner by ruthless hounds and she was standing her ground, sleek, vibrant, and beautiful like a treed panther. She would not be taken easily.

Dan, observing Connie's obduracy and not wanting to waste time, decided to destroy her resistance by delivering at the onset what he called his knockout punch, the coup de grace of Mormon arguments, the deification of Joseph Smith. "Please sit down, dear Sister," he said, "and let's allow the Spirit to be our mediator." He did not like her standing and him sitting. A woman should never be elevated over a man.

"I prefer to stand," she replied, aware that by standing it implied that she had not made them fully welcome. Besides, she could see that it made them uncomfortable.

"Connie," Dan began, mustering to the surface what little humility he possessed, "do you believe in Joseph Smith?"

Emma had thus far remained silent and continued to remain silent but gagged at that question. How many times had that same question been asked her at the dances by horny men like Seth, intent upon snaring her.

"If you mean," said Connie, "do I believe Joseph Smith really existed and was the man who organized the Mormon Church, yes."

Ah hah, thought Dan, as long as she answers my questions, I have her. "Do you also believe he was a prophet of God and that the revelations in the Doctrine & Covenants are commandments from God?"

"I assume, Brother Dan, that you are referring to the 132nd Section of the Doctrine & Covenants, the revelation that addresses the doctrine of plural marriage?" He nodded.

Connie replied, "The LDS Church abandoned polygamy and apparently for good reason. Furthermore, I have been taught not to trust in the arm of flesh, that if I have a question I should pray about it and receive my own confirmation. I have prayed many times about living polygamy today and have not received a burning of the bosom or any answer whatsoever."

"That is what the priesthood is for, to answer those questions. God will not let us lead you astray. Let me bear to you my testimony."

"Save your breath," said Connie, "I don't need your testimony to determine the truth."

"CONNIE!' Gene shouted and ran a hand through his hair. "Do you know who you're talking to?"

Dan held his hand up for Gene to be silent and let him deal with Connie.

Emma got up and walked over next to her mother and put her arm around her waist to show that she was solidly behind her. Connie returned the gesture. They were of even height, the younger a replica of the older, beautiful in defiance, regal, sure-footed and unyielding.

"Then, dear sister, what in Lord's name are you doing here?" Dan struggled to control his temper. He had not had a women challenge him like this. It was a blatant act of apostasy to defy or question the priesthood. He wanted to unleash his fury and give her what-for, but there was the money at stake. He had to remain calm.

"I promised Gene I would give the principle a try for a year. It has been over a year and I have received no testimony or seen anything endearing about it either for myself or my children. I am worse off now than before, and I'm expected to labor and give my talents to a priesthood that gives nothing in return but a pat on the back and idle promises of which there is no guarantee."

Don, who had yielded to Dan's seniority, jumped into the fray. "Your reward will be greater for trusting in the priesthood," he said humbly. "You cannot receive a celestial exaltation without the priesthood. That's why we're here, to save you from making a terrible mistake.

"Neither you nor your children will remain a family in heaven. At best, you will be confined to a place there reserved for the godless and unfaithful. And if you turn your back on the Holy Spirit, you will be cast into outer darkness and your very soul will cease to exist. Is this what you want for yourself and your children? Do you not see the need for the priesthood and its authority?" He paused for emphasis.

"What is sealed on earth shall be sealed in heaven. The priesthood can save you or damn you. We want to save you."

"In other words," said Connie facetiously, "if I pay my tithing and consecrate the remainder of my commission to the community leaders, the priesthood can guarantee my celestial exaltation?"

"That's right."

"No, thank you," Connie chuckled and pulled Emma closer. "I'll take my chances on my own. I've gotten along just fine so far without the priesthood."

"What about the resurrection?" interjected Dangerous Dan. "How do you expect to be resurrected without the priesthood?"

Connie looked down at Dan. "As long as we are laying everything on the table, in all due respect, I don't believe you hold any priesthood, and I certainly don't believe you have any power over the resurrection."

Gene could see everything he had worked for going down the drain.

"You are out of harmony with the priesthood," said Dan forcefully. "You have brought disgrace to your husband and sister-wife. You will all have to leave the community, forthwith."

"You mean you would evict Gene and Colleen because of my rebellion. What kind of priesthood is that?"

"It's in the occupancy agreement," said Don.

"If you even try to evict Gene and Colleen against their will, I'll spend every cent of my commission taking you and your priesthood to court," said Connie, not hiding her disgust. "I have a copy of that occupancy agreement and have showed it to my lawyer. He would just love to test it in court so the world will know just what kind of a tyrannical, medieval, communistic priesthood you really are."

"You can't stay," said Don. "You're no longer welcome."

"What makes you think I want to stay?" answered Connie. "I'll be out of here tomorrow. And now gentlemen, if you'll kindly leave, we'll start packing."

The two apostles got to their feet. Gene remained seated. Connie said, "You better go with them Gene, we can talk later."

Dangerous Dan's face turned grim and foreboding, a ruthlessness appeared that frightened Emma. The front door was open, but before Dan stepped out into the cold he turned to face Connie and with glaring, steel-gray eyes said, "To defy the priesthood and turn your back on the principle is to choose eternal damnation. Your only hope for redemption is to have your blood spilled. You would be wise to prostrate yourself on the alter of God and let His priests slit your throat and open up your bowels. May God have mercy on you soul."

"GET OUT!" cried Emma. Dan just stood there, defiant and smiling. Emma screamed, "You evil man, get out!" Humiliated, Gene took him by the arm and gently pushed him through the door.

Suddenly, Don popped his head back into the door. "I don't suppose you'd be interested in investing in my condo?"

Emma rushed to the door and slammed it in his face.

After they had gone, Emma apologized, "I'm sorry I screamed Mom. I couldn't help it."

"I understand," said Connie. "I wanted to scream myself. I've never been so mad in my life." She started pacing up and down the living room floor and then noticed Keith standing in the hallway.

"Where are we going to go, Mom?" he asked. And then he walked up to his mother and put an arm around her waist.

She messed his hair. "I've already taken care of that," she said cheerfully. "I've rented a house two blocks from your school. We'll stay there until school ends and then we're moving to the big city."

"ALL RIGHT!" shouted Keith with a large grin.

"Mom, you always knew what you were going to do, didn't you?" said Emma. "You never intended to give the priesthood any of that money."

"No, I didn't," confessed Connie. "I needed time to talk to attorneys, find a place for us to stay, and a dozen other things."

"You know," said Emma, "they're going to say you're greedy, that you're wicked, and who knows what else. They'll say anything rotten or filthy they can invent."

"I know it, but we know different. Don't we."

Tears swelled in Emma's eyes. She embraced her mother, holding her tightly. "Mom," she whispered. "I'm so proud of you."

Epilogue

When you're busy and the future unfolds as planned except for a few surprises that add spice to the adventure of life; when mountains are conquered and each new valley is more fertile and verdant than the last, time passes swiftly like a swallow slicing through an azure sky. The conquerors, the ones who overcome obstacles and who make things happen, don't look back or dwell on the past. They savor the present making every second count and keep an opportunistic eye focused on the future. Life is good to the conqueror, the adventurer, that person who is not afraid to step outside the security of his world. He does not tiptoe through life banking on luck or blaming others for failures. He makes his own way without ruthlessly exploiting the frailties of the naive and less fortunate, nor does he dine on food produced or provided by servants. The doers and givers of society are the adhesive stabilizers of the culture.

Ten years shot by as Emma, Bruce, Gwen, Mary, and the others drifted apart and eventually went their own way.

Gwen, true to form, chose wisely. During her second year at the University of Utah she met the man of her dreams, a returned missionary in dental school. They married a year later. Gwen's husband went on to become an orthodontist. He gave Gwen all a wife could expect and more—a home in an affluent neighborhood, travel, love, respect, and he took her through the LDS Temple where they were sealed for time and all eternity. She gave him three beautiful children, two daughters and a son. [7]

Bruce had planned to marry Mary's little sister, Sally, who thought if Mary could go out into the world, so could she. But she changed her mind. Bruce was committed to leaving polygamy behind and married a girl from another group. They too joined the

LDS Church. Bruce continued to build houses. His reputation as an honest, conscientious contractor spread and he was never without work. He built his wife the largest residence in the neighborhood. At last count they had six children.

Musically talented Susan bore her lawyer husband a retarded son. He blamed her and made her life miserable, physically pushing her around until she lost all self-esteem. She begged the priesthood for a release but they turned her down. Only when she attempted suicide did they give her a bill of divorcement. A year later, after recovering under her mother's care, she joined another family with a kind husband and supportive sister-wives. She sings at all their special occasions.

Lillian stayed faithful to Seth. As it turned out, Seth served two years before being paroled. It had something to do with marijuana that was found in his locker. Seth told the parole board someone framed him. As a condition of his parole, Seth abandoned the oil exploration and securities business and went back to his old occupation, building apartments and houses. Richard Partridge arranged for him to go into partnership with another contractor in the group. After a year the business went bankrupt. Each blamed the other. But men like Seth are hard to keep down. He bounced back, still in the contracting business, and is now building a mansion with an apartment for each wife. Seth finally found a fifth wife, and she works at Lillian's dress shop.

After ten years, Roger was still the recognized nemesis of the Partridge group. Actually, they needed him because all cults need people or groups to hate; it unifies their followers. Roger fit the bill perfectly and tried his best to accommodate them with every opportunity. Children in the group grew up being taught to hate all those on the "hate" list: Roger maintained his standing at the top of that list, then came the LDS Church, the United States Government, Tapestry Against Polygamy, the gentiles, the Jews, the communists, and at the bottom of the list were a few individuals of the same nature as Roger.

Gene struggled after Connie left. Finally, when he denounced her rebellious actions to the entire group, the priesthood forgave him, but watched him closely for two years fearing he might follow his insurrectional wife. When they were confident that he was a "cut and dried acolyte," they gave him another wife, then another, and another until his home was filled with crying babies and stinky diapers.

He labored diligently at being a good husband and there was no better father and family builder in the group. He worked from dawn to dark earning a living, arbitrating jealously disputes, repairing and remodeling the Four-Plex, fixing broken-down automobiles, and conspiring with his priesthood buddies how to make more money to support his big family. His reward was the affection of four ladies and a bumper crop of kids, and of course, the promise that he would evolve into a king, priest, ruler of men and God of his own worlds, one for each wife.

After Emma graduated from high school, Connie moved to a small town in northern Utah County where she paid cash for a house and invested the balance of her commission. Connie continued to do well selling real estate and after her third year was selected as one of the ten top Realtors of the year.

As a Realtor, Connie brushed shoulders with people at all levels, some of them very influential. With her intrinsic beauty, brains, and charm, she found herself hobnobbing with well known politicians, lawyers, prominent doctors, newspaper editors, college professors, and successful businessmen. She was where the action was and the contacts she made multiplied her sales.

Connie was not without male companionship. Men of all ages and economics sought her out. Along the way she unintentionally broke a few hearts until she finally met her match, a well-to-do widower with an elegant home surrounded by pine and oaks overlooking Little Cottonwood Creek. They married. He idolized her and smothered her with gifts and attention.

Gene did not see his son Keith play high school football, run for touchdowns, or knock two home runs in one game. He missed seeing him grow up to manhood, enter the Naval Academy, attend flight school, and graduate at the top of his class. But Connie and Emma were there, bursting with pride, snapping pictures of Keith in his navy blue uniform, white hat, and silver wings pinned to his chest.

Gwen and Mary lived with Connie and Emma for six months until they could afford an apartment of their own. Mary, encouraged by her experiences at Lillian's dress shop, applied for and received a grant, pending approval of a scholarship, and enrolled at Westminster College to pursue a nursing career. Her newfound freedom was both exhilarating and frightening for Mary, but with the urging of both Gwen and Emma, she marched on.

Before Emma had completed four quarters at the University of Utah, she was offered a scholarship at the University of Colorado, an offer she couldn't turn down. The three girls promised each other they would stay in touch. Saying goodbye, Emma told Mary how proud she was of her and the new life she had made. But as time passed, she lost contact with her friends

After graduation, Emma made her home in Denver where she married a professor of anthropology with a minor in archeology. He specialized in Middle Eastern cultures. His work took him on frequent sabbaticals to Egypt, Jordan, and Israel, where Emma and her two children, a boy and girl, frolicked in the Mediterranean.

But Emma was not cut out as a total housewife. She was also a writer and the urge to express ideas and thoughts cried out. She found employment as a feature editor and writer for a leading monthly magazine, and there her talents burst forth like sky rockets. Life couldn't have been better. Her children were healthy, she and her husband were still madly in love, enjoying each other, and each was doing the things they liked most. Life for Emma flowed smoothly and she was very, very happy.

Twice a year Emma and her children flew to Salt Lake City for a visit. Emma and Connie were very close. Weekly telephone conversations between the two became a ritual.

During one visit to Connie's, Emma and the kids were

thumbing through an old photo album, Emma talking about her youth. There was the old gang at girls camp—Gwen and Mary, clothes soaked after the tug-o-war, Lillian eating a hotdog, mustard on her chin. Emma sighed. It had been years since she had thought of her old friends. In retrospect, that year with the polygamists had been something special as well as a nightmare. She had stuffed the experience on a shelf somewhere in the back of her mind. But now memories gushed to the surface and she was caught in a fit of melancholy.

Haunted by the past, Emma thought of looking up her old friends or maybe calling them on the telephone. But they too had lives and she assumed, families. Maybe she would be an intrusion, a sore reminder of an unpleasant past. But then she thought of the fun, the dances, and how they helped each other through difficult times. She recalled the night Mary called her on the telephone, the despair and loneliness in her voice. But then she recalled that day in Lillian's shop when Mary landed her first job and how pretty she looked in her new dress. And she remembered the Saturday night at the dance when she first saw her father with Colleen. Tears welled in her eyes. How could she ever thank Mary, Gwen, and Bruce for the comfort they gave her?

She decided on the spur of the moment to borrow her mother's car and drive past some of the old places, like Lillian's dress shop. Excited, she decided she wouldn't stop or go in, just drive by for old time's sake. But she couldn't help herself. She stopped and raced in the door.

But Lillian was on a vacation to New York with Seth. A young girl that Emma presumed was Seth's new wife gave her an update on Lillian and it sounded like the Lillian she knew and loved. Nostalgia swept over Emma as she looked around the shop. Lillian had taught her about being a woman, had painted a picture of a female world Emma only guessed at. Truly, she owed Lillian a great deal. Emma reluctantly left, telling the salesgirl to mention to Lillian that she had been by.

Next she drove out to the polygamist community. From a distance she could see it had tripled in size and new multifamily dwellings were under construction. She tried to make out her father's Four-Plex, but it was hidden by other dwellings. That old yearning for her dad gripped her heart. But those days were gone, archived in her childhood. Emma felt little connection with the half brothers and sisters she knew lived nearby. For when they left the Partridge polygamist group, she had firmly closed the door. It was a world that only represented heartache. It was there she lost her father.

The high school was unchanged. The house they had rented and enjoyed when they left the group was now rundown with junk cars parked on the front lawn.

Memories of years past flooded her mind, returning her to a world she had long forgotten, a world she wanted no part of. Taking a deep breath, Emma decided to return home where she belonged, where she felt free.

As she drove past the local grocery store she decided to stop and purchase a six-pack of Pepsi, hamburger, and some buns for a barbecue.

As she pushed her cart toward the check stand, a women approached with three small children hanging on her dress. She was obviously a polygamist. Her dress was plain, long sleeved, and ankle length. The woman's lusterless brown hair was combed and tied back.

Poor thing.

The woman's eyes were lowered, her basket half full. Emma quickly but discretely scanned the contents—beans, flour, potatoes, rice, macaroni.

Emma thought the woman looked familiar and racked her brain. Was she from the community? Had they gone to school together? She had the facial characteristics of one of the blue blood families. And then they were side by side. Emma froze in her tracks. The blood drained from her face.

She blurted, "Mary, is that you?"

At that moment, if Emma could live the day over she would never have gone on that drive. And she would never had gone into the grocery store and if she had, she would have walked right past Mary as if she were a total stranger.

Mary stopped and gazed into Emma's face, saying nothing, registering nothing.

"Mary, it's me, Emma," she stammered, the words catching in her throat. "It's been so long, I hardly recognized you."

A weak, polite smile formed on Mary's face. "Why Emma, it's nice to see you. How have you been?" There was no enthusiasm in her voice. The sparkle in her blue eyes had dimmed.

Emma didn't know what to say. The last time she saw Mary, she was a sweet, beautiful girl with newfound freedom and plans to become a nurse in a children's hospital. Sweet, gentle, kind Mary.

Emma's heart broke. Before her stood a women old beyond her years. What could she say? But she *had* to know what had happened.

"The last time I saw you, Mary," said Emma carefully, "you were enrolled at Westminister College."

"I know. I'm sorry, Emma. I ... I just couldn't do it. I felt like an imposter. It just wasn't me. I finally had to face the truth ... I was wrong to try and leave the group. I tried, really I did ... but I didn't fit in. Without you and Gwen, I just didn't have what it takes. I'm sorry."

Emma fought back tears. "Oh, Mary, Mary ... I should have been there when you needed me."

"I don't blame you," said Mary compassionately. It was the first time she showed any emotion. "And please don't blame yourself. It was something I had to do on my own and just couldn't. I'm back where I belong." There was no regret in her voice, she was merely acknowledging a fact.

Emma wanted to scream, NO, YOU BELONG OUT IN THE WORLD, FREE, MAKING A LIFE.

"Is there still a chance, Mary? I'll help you. I promise ... this time I won't let you down."

Mary reached out and touched Emma's arm. "No, thank you. If I didn't have the strength when I was eighteen, I wouldn't have it now."

"Are you sure, Mary?"

Mary heaved a big sigh and pulled the youngest child close to her side. "From the day I was born," she said, "I was taught that I would grow up to be a plural wife. I was told it was the greatest calling a woman could have. I was told only a man holding the priesthood could resurrect me and take me to the celestial kingdom. And I was told that the outside world was Babylon and if I left the group, I would be damned. But … I think the real reason I didn't make it was the uncertainty. Emma, I was scared to death all the time … I just couldn't shake it."

One of Mary's daughters tugged on her dress, "Mommy, are we ready to go? I'm hungry." She was a pretty little thing, about five, a replica of her mother, soft pale skin and large blue eyes. Mary patted her on the cheek and said, "In just a minute, dear."

Looking back at Emma, Mary said, "The outside world was too much for me. I thought I could do it, I really did. I don't know how to be assertive, I never learned how to use my wits … and that's what it takes. In the group I don't have to worry about that … I don't have to try and fit in, I don't have to pass any tests, they accept me as I am. It finally came to me late one night … it's the only way I know how to live."

Swallowing hard against the outrage consuming her, Emma quietly inquired, "Are you living in the community?"

"No, I live on the West Desert Ranch in Snake Valley. I have a trailer."

Emma's mind flashed to the West Desert Ranch, several thousand acres of alfalfa and sage brush, 125 miles from the nearest paved road. Besides the elaborate ranch, there were three other homes and a dozen trailer houses, some so rundown they looked ready to collapse. This is where the priesthood elite stuck their third, fourth, or fifth wives because it was cheap. Every two or three weeks the women got to come to town for a visit and purchase groceries. The ranch was a great place for children to run and play, but it was isolation for young mothers.

"Oh, Mary, I'm worried about you," Emma whispered. "Are you okay? Do you have enough? Can I get you something?"

One of the little girls spoke up, "We have food stamps." Her tone of voice said food stamps was something special.

"Thank you again, but no, we're just fine." Mary hesitated for a second, and then said, "Well, Emma, I must finish my shopping. It's a long drive back to the ranch. It was really nice to see you."

Emma watched Mary and the children until they reached the end of the aisle. She waited for Mary to look back over her shoulder, wave and smile, a sign that they were still friends. But she didn't.

Emma's legs were quivering. *I've got to get out of here.* She abandoned her grocery cart and rushed outside. "Without you and Gwen there ..." resounded in her head over and over. She had difficulty breathing. Slipping into her car, she gripped the steering wheel hard to try and calm herself.

If only I had known. If only I could turn back the clock. If only I had stayed here.

Her guilt became unbearable. She wanted to race to her mother's house. A second later she wanted to find Richard Partridge and scratch his eyes out. Anything ... anything to relieve the guilt she was feeling.

Mary came out of the grocery store, the cart holding two brown bags, the children tagging behind. Stopping at an old blue minivan coated with red dust, she opened the rear lid and the children carefully removed the contents of the cart and placed them gently in the back of the van. The precious sacks were treated by the children as if they contained gold.

My children would toss the groceries into the car knowing if an egg broke or the bread got smashed, there's always more at the grocery store.

Watching Mary drive down the highway out of sight, Emma floored the accelerator toward her mother's house. Racing in the door, she fell into her mother's lap, telling her everything between sobs. "I should never have gone to Denver. Oh Mom, what have I done ...."

Connie let her get it all out. Then she took Emma's hands and looked deep into her eyes.

"My darling, you and Mary belong to two different worlds," and she paused for a moment.

"When I was a little girl my parents had a canary, a pretty little bird with yellow feathers. I felt sorry for it, all cooped up, so I took it outside to turn it loose. I just knew it would be happier to be free. So I opened the cage door ... but it wouldn't fly out. Finally I reached inside, grabbed it, and tossed it up in the air. Guess what happened. That little canary flew right back inside the cage. You see, that was the only life the canary knew. I can see that now. To him it was his security."

"But, Mom …"

"Emma … Mary doesn't want you to feel sorry for her. You need to let Mary go as she has let you go."

They sat in silence while Emma let her mother's wisdom sink in.

"Mom … I know in my head that you're right. But I simply can't bear it."

"Darling, you have no choice but to accept this."

"But I've got to do something, anything. I cannot bear knowing Mary and her little girls will never have a life … never develop what's inside them desperate to burst forth and blossom. So few are strong like Lillian. And maybe, Mom, maybe it was her dad's abuse that finally robbed Mary of what strength she had. You know, experts say that sexual abuse can cripple a girl. And think how it must have affected Mary, believing as she did in the godly authority of her own father …. Her very foundation must have shattered."

Connie patiently listened.

"You know, Mom, for ten years I have compartmentalized polygamy, the good and the bad, I've put it clear out of my mind. I am a writer, a good writer and yet I haven't written one word about polygamy. I guess I was too ashamed of our involvement. But you know … it's time I wrote something.

"The world absolutely must know about these women, that they start out just like other women in their loves and fears, their needs and wants. That they have hopes, dreams, and desires just like the rest of us. Just like Mary did …" Emma's voice broke.

"Maybe … maybe through writing, I can tell the world about polygamy and bring it out of its terrible secrecy. Maybe it could pave the way for those who want out. And for women like Lillian who want to stay because it works for them, they should be treated with respect. I honestly believe if the secrecy stopped, polygamist women and children could stop hiding. If they were made more welcome by society, had a chance to really experience the world, they would eventually gain some freedom from the domination of cult leaders. If we could Americanize the mothers, in time they will

Americanize the children … there would be no way to stop it.

"Mom, I've thought about it all the way home. If Mary had at least gone to a public school she *would* have become stronger, more sure of herself. It would have given her a real chance to see how other people live, to experience the outside world early enough in her life to have made a difference."[8]

Connie listened to her daughter with pride—and gratitude. Emma would do more than have a good life. She would make a difference.

And what if I had never left?

NOTES

1. *The Deseret News*, November 14, 1855. 1.

2. Hyrum Andrus, *Doctrines of the Kingdom*, (Salt Lake City: Bookcraft, 1973), 439. Joseph Smith's plural marriage announcement was publicly introduced in Nauvoo sometime around 1842 or 1843.

3. *In Sacred Loneliness, The Plural Wives of Joseph Smith*, Signature Books, 1997, Todd Compton. 4-8.

4. The purposefully subdued portrayal of sexual abuse in *A Teenager's Tears* is included to illustrate the far reaching impact upon a child when such events occur, the complexities of having been taught unquestioning belief in the authority of such a priesthood holder, and the resulting conflicts created regarding one's belief in God.

Rena Mackert, who shared her story on A&E TV Documentary "Inside Polygamy" and also for this book, was the victim of a psychopathic, pedophilic father. As children, she and her siblings were taught to pray when in danger and God would come to their assistance. She and her sisters were repetitively ravished by their conscienceless, depraved father. They would lie in bed and hear his footsteps advancing down the hallway.

Contorted with panic, they would feverishly pray for God to come to their rescue. When the evil, paternal works of the pedophile-father were laid out in blazing truth before the prophet, pious, infallible Roy Johnson, he scolded and damned Rena for threatening to destroy the reputation of a "good righteous" man, a loyal member of Roy Johnson's eternal priesthood. And so it is with all polygamist cults: preserve the feigned integrity of the priesthood, even at the expensive of helpless children.

Rena states, "Organized polygamy is organized crime."

Laura Chapman, Rena Mackert's sister, has appeared on several TV documentaries, including ABC's 20/20, CBS 48 Hours, and A&E's "Inside Polygamy" exposing the dark side of contemporary cultic, organized polygamist machinations.

Their heroic candor has produced death threats, resulting in their precautionary emigration to outlying states. In spite of the threats, they have resolved to tell the truth when queried.

Pedophilia is an ugly blight present in all the organized groups. It is my opinion based on my law enforcement experience and personal observations that due to the nature and structure of polygamist societies, (secrecy, intimacy of large families in closed quarters, male authoritative figure, female subservience, etc.) sexual perversions are more apt to surface and resurface than in monogamous societies. A pedophile is cursed with strong feelings of inadequacy. His victims, children, do not detect those feelings of inadequacy, permitting the pedophile to perform competently. Many pedophiles develop a super-god ego where they feel they have power over life and death. He is a good psychologist and often seeks occupations or hobbies where he comes in contact with children. Because of the authoritative and humbling aspects of organized polygamist sects, it is a favorable environment for pedophiles.

—Author John Llewellyn pioneered the Morals Squad of the Sheriff Department, which handled the investigation of polygamous complaints. He also wrote a sex crimes manual for the Utah State Police Academy, where he taught Sex Crime Investigation, Interview, and Interrogation.

5. The author estimates that of the sister-wives in the least oppressive group upon which this novel is largely based, and those who are independents, fifty percent have good relationships with one another. Many are biological sisters and most have been raised in the polygamous lifestyle.

6. *The Salt Lake Tribune* article, "Couple Fight Eviction by Religious Group" by Hilary Groutage Smith, Aug. 23, 2000, tells

the story of one family facing eviction from their home because they refuse a priesthood-directed order for a polygamous marriage of their sixteen-year-old daughter to a thirty-nine year old man.

7. The author reports that the LDS Church greatly desires to rescue the Fundamentalists, convert them to true doctrine, and have them return to full fellowship within the Church.

8. As of this writing, the media reports that the leader of one of the most oppressive polygamous groups has commanded that all of its children presently in the public school system must drop out and attend the group's private school or be home schooled. Additionally, he has commanded that any of their members who are teachers in the public school system must resign their jobs.

Members are commanded they must sever all ties with family or friends not in the group. It is reported that leaders recently chastised girls for ignoring the dress code of high collars, long skirts, and no pierced ears or makeup. Over the last twelve months, a half-dozen teenagers have been arrested for alcohol or tobacco violations, and reports about runaways continue. Some experts believe the leaders are fearful the next generation will be lost to the modern world or to the mainstream Church of Jesus Christ of Latter-day Saints, which disavowed polygamy 110 years ago.

Mike King, special investigator for the Utah attorney general and whose work a decade ago led to the arrest and conviction of polygamous child abuser Arvin Shreeve, stated that the tactics of this group come down to dominion, control and power.

PUBLISHER NOTE

In the February 2000 session of the Utah State Legislature, a law was passed raising the minimum age for a legal marriage from fourteen to sixteen, and the law stipulated that a child age sixteen to eighteen must have parental consent to marry.

In the February 2001 session of the Utah Legislature, Senator Ron Allen, D-Stansbury Park, Utah, sponsored Senate Bill 146 to make it a third degree felony for parents or pastors to condone or solemnize outlawed marriages of minors. Douglas White, attorney for Tapestry Against Polygamy, helped write SB146 specifically targeting polygamist marriages involving children not of legal age to marry.

The proposed legislation sparked opposition from the polygamist subculture and an estimated one hundred polygamy advocates converged on Utah's Capital Hill to voice their opposition at various committee hearings. Most notable were:

Sidney Anderson, director of the Women's Religious Liberty Union, WRLU, an organization composed of bold polygamist women.

Owen A. Allred, leader of the second largest polygamist group, The Corporation of the Presiding Elder of Apostolic United Brethren, AUB.

Mary Batchelor, Marianne Watson and Anne Wilde– compilers of the recently privately printed book *Voices In Harmony*, a celebration of plural marriage by plural wives. They recently decided to go public and have gained favorable publicity.

The public appearance of a large number of polygamists is unprecedented. The primary credit for organizing this protest goes to independent polygamist Sidney Anderson of the WRLU. She persuaded polygamist leader Owen A. Allred to make his unprecedented public appearance before the legislature. The protesting polygamists are among the more liberal and open-minded of Mormon fundamentalists, but represent half or less of the polygamist subculture. These particular polygamists are as opposed to forced child marriages as are monogamists; and they are concerned about the preservation of their subculture.

In a Capital Hill committee meeting, Vickie Prunty, Executive Director of Tapestry Against Polygamy, offered to produce documentary evidence of unlawful child marriages that have occurred within the Fundamentalist LDS Church, headquartered in Colorado City, Arizona.

Both sides were invited to choose one person to summarize their support of or opposition to the proposed legislation:

Sidney Anderson represented the polygamists and said they could live with the bill if solemnizing unlawful marriages between consenting adults was changed from a felony to a misdemeanor.

Author John Llewellyn, former law enforcement officer and former polygamist was invited by Vicky Prunty and Douglas White to represent their position. He told the gathering there was a serious problem in polygamy with marketing young girls as plural wives, the bill addressed that issue, it was a good bill and would tend to strike at the pocket book of the men who market the solemnizing of plural marriages for recognition of priesthood authority and monetary tithes.

After a few revisions, a House judiciary committee unanimously passed the measure to the House floor. Those revisions included 1) softening a provision targeting religious leaders who solemnize outlawed marriages of "consenting adults"; that crime now would be a misdemeanor. 2) Also removed was language that would make it a felony for parents to promote or encourage polygamy.

The Utah House of Representatives voted and passed Senate Bill 146, which makes the solemnization of an unlawful marriage with a minor a third degree felony.

SB146 also makes it a Class A misdemeanor for anyone to solemnize a marriage prohibited by law.

". . . In the end, opposing sides accepted SB146 as a palatable way to protect young girls. . . . 'We are very pleased with the steps forward that this bill is taking,' said Sidney Anderson.. . . 'Our policy of ignoring and shunning polygamy for 100 years has not solved the problem,' Allen said. 'It's got to start with dialogue.' . . .

"Also watching was Ellery Kingston, a member of the polygamous Kingston clan. One of Kingston's cousins was recently convicted of incest with a 16-year-old girl forced to become his 15th wife. The girl's father was convicted for beating the girl when she attempted to flee the incestuous marriage. The case is a prime example of the behavior Allen hopes to dissuade. . . ."

"Polygamists Claim Partial Victory" Greg Burton, *Salt Lake Tribune*, Feb. 17, 2001.

"A measure aimed at curbing teen-age marriages in polygamous communities passed the House 71-0 Wednesday. . . . The bill would make it a felony for parents or pastors to condone or solemnize outlawed marriages of minors. . . ."

"Curbing Teen Marriages Gets House Approval" Greg Burton, *Salt Lake Tribune*, Feb 22, 2001.

What significance will this legislation have on the polygamist subculture? In the opinion of this author, possibly little because the subculture is too well rooted. The secret polygamist societies will become more secret. Yes, the bill was needed and sends a message both to polygamists and the world. But the cost of enforcing it, if it's enforced, will be monumental. But it is a beginning. The key to liberating oppressed women and children in the polygamist cults lies with the women.

The drama played on Capital Hill has been by women. The wives have stepped out and taken the lead. Sidney Anderson has offered to work with Tapestry Against Polygamy in helping combat abuse to children in polygamy. Even the compilers of *Voices In Harmony* now concede that there are serious problems in the subculture that are more than occasional.

Most of the women and children Tapestry has helped have been those with the courage to leave on their own. But it is the brainwashed mother and daughter who would like to leave but don't know how, that need the help. Tapestry Against Polygamy has not been trusted by most polygamist women, but the WRLU can help solve that problem and they can work together. Also women within polygamy are "insiders" and can more effectively get the civil rights message to the secret societies of Colorado City and the Kingston Group.

In essence, it is a golden opportunity for both sides to promote the clean up of the corruption in the subculture, primarily the marketing of young girls as wives.

Governor Michael Leavitt is expected to sign the bill.

Printed in the United States
200916BV00013B/157-186/A